DIGGING DEEPER

DIGGING DEEPER

Investigations into

ROCKS, SHOCKS, QUAKES, and OTHER EARTHY MATTERS

SANDRA MARKLE

Lothrop, Lee & Shepard Books
New York

I would especially like to thank Dr. Gerald H. Krockover
for sharing both his expertise and his enthusiasm.

—S.M.

First Edition   1 2 3 4 5 6 7 8 9 10

Library of Congress Cataloging in Publication Data   Markle, Sandra.   Digging deeper.
Includes index. Summary: Discusses various aspects of geology, such as plate tectonics, erosion, and mineral resources. Includes related experiments and activities.
   1. Geology—Juvenile literature. [1. Geology] I. Title.   QE31.M266 1987   550
86-27412   ISBN 0-688-05986-4

*For my daughter, Holly,
who always finds the best rocks.*

Contents

Ready, Set . . .

Looking at your home planet from out in space gives you a unique view. The swirled clouds are proof that there is an atmosphere. From here it only looks like a thin film, but it's really hundreds of miles thick. Most of what you can see below the clouds is water. You can pick out the Atlantic, the Pacific, the Indian, the Arctic, and the Antarctic oceans. Look closer, and you'll see that these are actually connected, forming one global ocean. It covers approximately 70 percent of the planet's surface. Maybe your home should have been called *water* instead of earth.

Those puzzle-piece shapes are land. You can recognize North America. There is Greenland, the world's largest island. That's not a cloud at the southernmost part of the planet. That thick white mass is the mostly ice- and snow-covered continent of Antarctica. Fossils—traces of past life—found there helped to solve some mysteries about earth.

NASA

What you can't tell from space is that earth is a dynamic planet. Interaction between the air, the water, and the land is constantly changing the surface. Forces deep within the crust are at work too. Sometimes, such as when a volcano erupts, the results are sudden and dramatic. Or, as when a river cuts down through nearly 2 miles of rock, the changes may take millions of years. As you dig deeper, you'll explore what makes the earth's land masses have their ups and downs. You'll discover islands that have come and gone, land that is sinking, and some that has the shakes.

Do you know the one place in the United States to look for diamonds? Do you know why Niagara Falls won't last? Can you tell how old a rock is? Any idea where to go to make sandcastles on a green beach? If you want to find the answers to these questions and discover a whole lot more, stop hanging around out there in space. The action's right here on the planet itself. Dig in!

What happened to the earth in this picture? To find out, turn the page and start . . .

Investigating Forces That Shape and Build

U.S. Geological Survey

Earthquake!

The damage you saw in the picture was caused by the 1964 earthquake at Anchorage, Alaska. Earthquakes are a result of forces at work shaping and building up the earth's crust. This epic quake provided information that led to a major change in the theories explaining such forces. Never in recorded history had a single quake deformed such a large land area—more than 100,000 square miles. The area around Kodiak, Alaska, dropped 6 feet while Valdez, Alaska, rose 10 feet. Seward, Alaska, about 225 miles away, shifted 47 feet. The Kenai Penisula sank about 7 feet and moved sideways 60 feet. A new 1,000-foot-wide beach appeared where land offshore lifted nearly 30 feet.

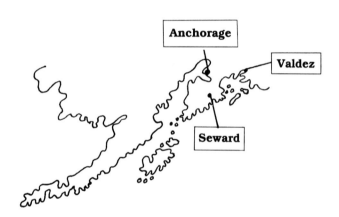

The Good Friday quake, as it was called because it fell on that religious holiday, was one of the strongest ever recorded, measuring 8.4 on the Richter scale (see Measuring Quakes, page 8). As the ground began to roll like ocean waves, streets in Anchorage split and heaved. Gas and water lines burst. Fortunately the city's main electrical generators and major gas lines had earthquake-activated switches and shut down, helping to prevent fires. Nothing stopped the collapsing buildings.

Masonry slabs 5 inches thick slipped off the face of the J.C. Penney store, crashing onto people fleeing into the streets. Windows shattered. Cars bounced along out of control. Crevasses, or giant cracks, opened. One end of the Government Hill Elementary School dropped 20 feet. Trees splintered and twisted. The 68-foot-tall concrete air traffic control tower at Anchorage International Airport toppled. At Turnagain Heights, a whole bluff of the city's best residential homes slipped into the churning sea. The air was full of the sounds of cracking, creaking, smashing disaster for nearly four minutes—a very long time for an earthquake. Such shaking events are normally measured in seconds.

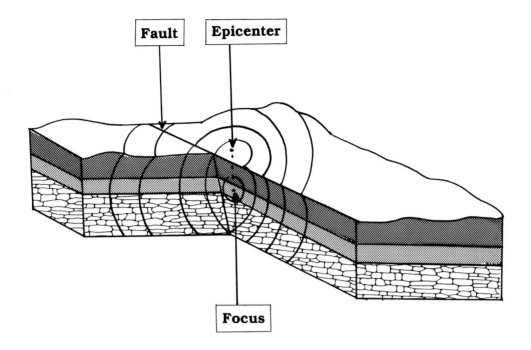

And the destruction wasn't over. Shock waves swept east at nearly 2 miles a second along Alaska's coast. To see how earthquake vibrations spread through the crust, put a small amount of water in a clear plastic cup. Stretch clear wrap tightly over the top and press the edges together to seal them. Then, working over a sink, turn the cup upside down so the water is resting on the clear wrap and gently tap the plastic with your finger. The *focus* of the earthquake, the point in the earth's crust where something happens to cause the quake, is like the spot you poked. The *epicenter* is the point on the earth's surface (the surface of the water) directly above the focus. Tap the clear wrap again a little more sharply. Can you see the effect of the shock waves moving outward to the sides of the glass? In the same way, vibrations from the Alaskan quake made water slosh in reservoirs, lakes, and swimming pools as far away as the Gulf of Mexico.

When the shock waves reached Seward, Alaska, a major oil port, pipelines broke, spewing oil. A spark ignited the fuel, and as the fire spread, twenty-six storage tanks full of petroleum erupted with the force of exploding bombs. Railroad tracks along the shore grew so hot they glowed, and flaming, oil-covered waves washed over the harbor.

At Valdez, 120 miles from Anchorage, on the edge of Prince William Sound, water and soft soil spouted 20 feet into the air from long cracks. Then the earth's rolling affected the water in the harbor the way you would scooting rapidly back and forth in your bathtub. Waves sloshed ashore, rolled back, and slammed into the land again with even greater force. A pier crowded with people who had come to welcome the S.S. *Chena* sank suddenly, and the 10,000-ton freighter was shoved inland over the dock. The lighthouse at Valdez Narrows was knocked off its 35-foot-high foundation.

National Oceanic and Atmospheric Administration

Late that evening, hours after the earth had stopped heaving, the final effect of the earthquake struck. *Tsunami*—giant ocean waves generated by shifts in the earth's crust deep underwater—slammed ashore. Kodiak had escaped major damage from the earthquake but was now hit hard by the surging sea. Many boats of a 160-boat fleet, along with buildings and docks, were swept inland to the center of Kodiak. At Valdez, the waters rushed up the narrows and flooded what was left of the already devastated village.

Although 115 people were killed and many millions of dollars' worth of property was destroyed by the earthquake, the damage and the death toll were relatively small. If such a major quake had struck a more densely populated area, the results would have been far worse.

Although the loss of life and property was sad, for *geologists*—people who study the earth—the Alaskan earthquake provided a unique opportunity for study. They rushed to survey and measure the spectacular changes. It was like clambering around on a life-size experiment, and for the first time geologists had a tool—electronic computers—capable of helping them analyze the data they collected. The computers could quickly sort and compare, find similarities and unique features. What the geologists wanted to discover was what forces had caused this to happen. There was also the hope that they could learn to understand these forces well enough to predict quakes—someday—with the kind of accuracy that allows communities to evacuate before hurricanes.

In the rest of the world, scientists had also been studying earthquakes. In the Soviet Union, geologists had already begun to compile data that would reveal patterns of earth activities related to quakes by moving into an area that had suffered two dramatically destructive earthquakes. The Chinese had installed an extensive network of earth-sensing instruments. Through a program of public preparedness and awareness, government officials in the People's Republic involved everyone in the search for "signs" and in getting ready to survive the next major quake. The Japanese effort included remote-controlled monitoring capsules on the ocean floor. The United States developed a worldwide network of more than 100 stations collecting information about forces at work in the earth. (This effort was in part motivated by the Defense Department's desire to determine the difference between vibrations generated by natural earthquakes and those resulting from secret, underground Russian nuclear bomb tests.)

Gradually, new theories were developed and a model was formed that explained the dynamic nature of the earth. Cautiously, these ideas have been used to make earthquake predictions—sometimes successfully. This information has also been used to help architects design buildings and public utility equipment that is better able to withstand quakes.

After the 1964 quake, town officials in Valdez, Alaska, sought the help of geologists as they planned for reconstruction. Using the information they received, city leaders decided to totally relocate Valdez rather than rebuild on the original site. Today Valdez is built on "safer ground."

Measuring Quakes

The ancient Greeks thought a giant named Atlas carried the world and when he shifted his heavy burden, there was an earthquake. The Japanese believed the earth rode on the back of a spider and that when the spider shook one of its feet, the earth quaked. Other similar versions of this story around the world gave the job of supporting the earth and causing quakes to a bull, an elephant, a tortoise, a dog, and a frog. Today geologists have developed a theory called *plate tectonics* that looks at how the pieces of the earth's crust interact and change to provide a logical explanation for what forces shape and build the earth's surface.

No one has yet been able to dig deep enough to observe firsthand what goes on under the earth's crust or even very far within the crust. Investigating earthquake waves is one of the few ways geologists have of learning about what's inside the earth. There are two main kinds of seismic, or earthquake, waves—*body waves*, which are transmitted through the interior of the earth, and *surface waves*, which travel along the surface.

Put your ear against a wooden table or door and tap on the wood with your fingers. Now repeat this, tapping on something metal (like the bottom of a pan). You're listening to sound waves being transmitted through two different kinds of matter. Hear the difference? In a similar way, studying body waves provides clues about the matter they are transmitted through. Geologists use special instruments called *seismographs* to record the body waves so they can be studied. There are two distinctly different types of body waves—*compressional waves*, also called primary or P waves, and *shear waves*, also called secondary or S waves.

Compressional waves cause particles of matter in the earth to move together and then spread apart behind them. To see a compressional wave in action, use the spring from an old spiral notebook or coil a piece of wire to make a spring. Hold one end of the metal spring in each hand. Alternately push one hand toward the other to compress the spring and then pull that hand back to stretch the coils. P waves can move through solids, liquids, and gases. They travel very fast—the denser the material, the more tightly the molecules are packed, the quicker these waves are transmitted. Compressional waves are also called primary waves because they are the first waves recorded by seismographs.

Shear waves cause particles to vibrate from side to side at right angles. To see how shear waves transfer energy, hold the metal spring in front of you with one end in each hand. Next, jerk your right hand away from your body and then quickly pull your hand back. Following your motion, the spring will swing out and back. If you could look down on the moving spring, you would see the shape of an S.

Shear waves travel through the earth more slowly than compressional waves and can't pass through liquids. Molecules in a liquid slide past each other rather than move apart in opposite directions in response to the shearing force.

Earthquakes are usually measured by one of two scales, the Richter scale or the Modified Mercalli scale. The Richter scale, named after Dr. Charles F. Richter, its developer, is based on the amplitude—the extreme range—of seismic waves as they are recorded on a seismograph. This measurement is then interpreted as a number representing the magnitude, or the intensity of the energy released, of the quake. A tremor measuring 2 is the lowest most people can recognize. However, really sensitive seismographs have measured quakes with a magnitude as low as minus 3. Earthquakes with a magnitude of 7 or greater are considered major quakes.

Using special travel-time graphs, the distance from a seismograph recording station to the epicenter of an earthquake can be determined using the difference in arrival times of the P and S waves. As you'll remember, earthquake waves travel out in all directions. So to locate the quake's origin, three or more stations must determine their distance from the epicenter and use this measurement to draw a circle around their location. The epicenter is the point where these circles intersect.

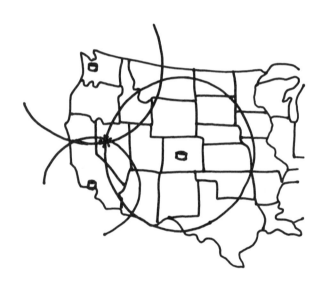

The Modified Mercalli scale, named after Giuseppe Mercalli, its developer, measures the intensity of earthquakes based on property damage and eyewitness accounts. Measurements are shown by Roman numerals on a scale of I to XII. Recently values of XIII through XVII have been added to cover really disastrous quakes. A tremor must rate a V before it's widely felt and any damage is done. On this scale, the 1964 Alaskan quake measured X. Most of the structural damage measured by the Modified Mercalli scale is caused by surface waves. These make the ground roll while it's being jerked side to side by a shearing force similar to that of S waves.

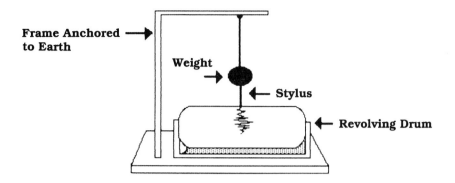

The seismograph has historically been the instrument geologists depended on to record earthquakes. This instrument works because of inertia, meaning that an object at rest tends to remain at rest unless acted upon by some outside force. A heavy weight on a spring is mounted on a base anchored in bedrock (rock below any weathered rock or soil). Vibrations traveling through the rock make the weight move—the stronger the bedrock displacement the greater the weight's response. This motion used to be recorded by a pen, but now a light beam on photographic paper or an electrical impusle records the motion. Three different seismographs are used together, measuring vertical movement, east-west movement, and north-south movement, to provide a complete record.

You can make your own model seismograph to see how this instrument works. (You may want an adult's help with this project.) You'll need:

wire cutters

a very flexible wire coat hanger

a hammer

three steel nails

a piece of plywood or a board at least 6 inches x 12 inches

a single-edge razor blade

a cereal box (medium-sized)

wide masking tape

a felt-tip pen

a tablespoon of modeling clay (an inch of a stick)

four sheets of plain white typing paper or continuous-feed
    computer paper

scissors

1. With the wire cutters, cut the hanger on either side of the hook. Bend one end of the wire, as shown, and hammer the nails partway into the board. Pound the nails all the way down to anchor the base of the wire onto the board.

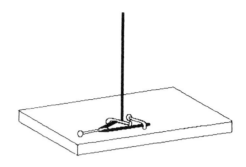

2. Use the razor blade to carefully cut a slot near the top on the front of the box. Make the slot about half an inch wide and long enough for a sheet of typing paper folded in half lengthwise to slip through easily. Cut a matching slot near the box bottom. Then cut two more slots, one opposite each of these, on the back. Tape the lid of the box shut. Use tape to anchor the box on the wood so that the wire is in the very center of the box.

3. Cut off and bend the top of the hanger wire to form a loop just big enough for the pen to slip through. Take off the cap and slide the pen into the loop. Press the clay around the pen to add weight and to hold the pen securely in place.

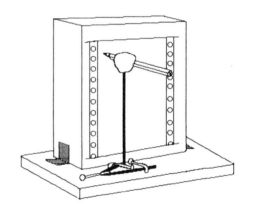

4. Cut the paper sheets in half lengthwise. Tape the ends together to form one long sheet. Thread the paper through the slots in the box as shown. Bend the wire so the tip of the pen just touches the paper.

5. Work with a friend. Set your seismograph on a table. While you slowly and steadily pull the paper through the upper slot from the back of the box, have your friend begin to vibrate the table. These vibrations should be gentle at first, become more violent, and then be more gentle again. Look at the recorded results. Can you tell when your simulated earthquake became stronger? How can you tell?

You may want to leave your seismograph set up, particularly

if you live in an area likely to have earthquakes. Remember, however, that your seismograph will record any kind of vibration—a subway train passing, a tree falling, or someone jumping. Real seismographs are also often affected by non-quake vibrations.

Geologists use a number of other instruments to detect changes resulting from forces at work within the earth. A *surveyor's level and a calibrated rod* detect changes in elevation—one portion of land moving up or down in relation to another. A *laser-ranging instrument* reveals the slightest horizontal movement across a fault (a crack in the earth) by measuring how long it takes light to travel from the pulsing device to a specific point and back. A *strainmeter* measures expansion and contraction of rocks caused by tension being increased or released. A *creepmeter* is stretched diagonally across a fault to register any horizontal movement. A *scintillator counter* determines the amount of radioactive radon gas in well water. Geologists have discovered that before a quake, rocks release this gas, causing the radon level in wells to increase dramatically. A *tiltmeter* works like a carpenter's level to reveal when the earth's surface tilts. A *magnetometer* records local changes in the earth's magnetic field. Such changes occur when rocks are deformed under pressure.

Watch Rats and Taste the Water

In the People's Republic of China, people are warned to watch for rats running from buildings, horses rearing, and dogs acting disturbed as possible signs that there is about to be an earthquake. Citizens are also told to notice any sudden changes in the level, clarity, and taste of well water. Bitter water can be a sign of increased amounts of radon gas.

How Likely Is a Quake?

Some parts of the United States are more likely to have earthquakes than others. To discover how great the risk of a quake is where you live, check the earthquake-risk map of the contiguous, or connected, United States (minus Alaska and Hawaii) below. The map is based on data about past quakes compiled by the U.S. Department of the Interior/Geological Survey. Notice that the areas with the greatest risk are mainly along either coast.

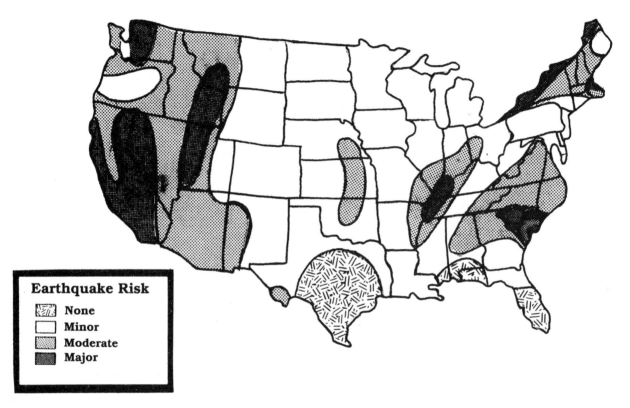

Earthquake Risk
- None
- Minor
- Moderate
- Major

No one is sure why there is a high-risk area in the middle of the United States. Very little is known about the location of active faults in this region because there have been very few earthquakes of sufficient strength to study since the early 1960s, when the number of earthquake measuring stations was greatly increased. However, probably the strongest quakes ever felt in North America were the 1811 and 1812 quakes that centered at New Madrid, Missouri. Vibrations reached as far as Massachusetts and South Carolina. The Mississippi River even briefly reversed the direction of its flow as a result of the most violent earth tremors.

Shaking Buildings

Today a "shaking table" lets *architects,* people who design buildings, find out in advance how their building will hold up. In 1932 scientists at the California Institute of Technology in Pasadena created an instrument called a *strong-motion accelerograph* (SMA) that could measure exactly how the ground was moving during a strong earthquake. They planted SMAs at six likely Southern California sites and waited. Finally, in 1940, a quake measuring 7.1 on the Richter scale struck El Centro, California, and the effect was recorded by an SMA. The shaking table these scientists created based on the El Centro quake was improved through the years. The current model is controlled by a computer and is capable of simulating a full range of destructive earthquake forces and construction site conditions.

The Transamerica Building in San Francisco, California, was specially designed and tested to withstand a quake as bad as the one that struck in 1906 (see page 22 for more information about this famous quake). The base of this 853-foot building is not only much wider than its peak, it has triangular trusses (supporting brackets) and reinforced concrete columns for additional strength.

Transamerica Corporation

Plate Tectonics

You can use a hard-boiled egg as a model of what geologists have determined the earth's internal structure must be like from studying body waves. Tap the egg on a table or other hard surface to crack the shell into a number of pieces. (Don't remove the shell.) Then place the egg on a paper towel, hold it with the pointed end up, and slice straight down from top to bottom with a regular table knife.

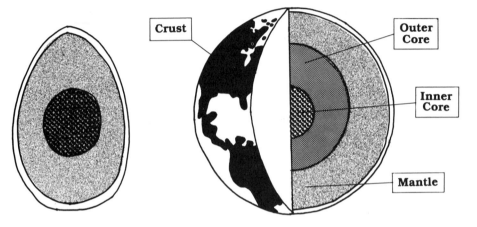

The egg yolk represents the *core* of the earth. Geologists believe that the core is composed of an iron and nickel material and made up of two layers—an inner core about 870 miles thick and an outer core about 1,300 miles thick. They think the inner core must be solid because both P and S waves pass through it. They think the outer core must be liquid or behave like a liquid because shear waves won't pass through it. Picture the outer portion of the yolk as being undercooked and runny. The core is believed to be responsible for the fact that the earth has a magnetic field, but no one is sure how this field is generated.

Because of this magnetic field, the earth has magnetic poles that are different from its geographic poles. Magnetic north is near Bathurst Island in northern Canada about 1,000 miles from the geographic North Pole. The north-seeking end of a compass needle points to magnetic north. You have to know how to correct for this difference to find geographic north and use a compass to find your way.

The white of the egg represents the *mantle.* This layer is thought to be about 1,789 miles thick and composed of silicon, magnesium, and iron. Geologists still haven't agreed on the consistency of the mantle. Some believe that this material may at times flow like a liquid in response to tremendous heat and pressure, but that it will break like a solid if moved suddenly. Others believe that the mantle is always fairly solid and that currents of energy flow through it.

Like the egg's shell, the earth's *crust* is a very thin, relatively light, rigid layer broken into a number of plates. The earth's crust ranges from 3 to about 31 miles thick. It's thickest under the highest mountains and thinnest under the ocean. Geologists refer to the crust combined with the uppermost portion of the mantle as the *lithosphere.* They call the area from about 43 to 186 miles below the surface the *asthenosphere.* This region is important because volcanic lavas are produced here, and unequal heating of the mantle material creates circulating currents that very slowly move the crustal plates.

Whether the mantle material actually moves or energy is only transferred through it, *convection currents* are created. You can see how convection currents form and circulate by boiling water in a pan on a stove. As soon as the water is bubbling, drop in a few raisins or grains of rice. Watch these objects cycle up, around, and down. The water is hottest closest to the heat source at the bottom of the pan. The hot water rises while cooler water near the surface sinks.

Geologists know from tests made inside deep mines and drill holes that the earth's temperature increases the deeper you go. They believe that the decay of radioactive elements in the earth generates this heat. However, like the heat source for the water you boiled, geothermal heat is not evenly distributed. For example, drill holes in Georgia several hundred feet deep registered temperatures very close to those recorded near the surface. At a hot spot like Yellowstone National Park, though, the temperature rose rapidly as the depth increased.

Geologists today believe that the forces that shape and build the earth's crust are a result of *plate tectonics.* This theory explains that the earth's crust is broken into a number of pieces that are moving and interacting in response to the convection currents going on deep inside the earth. At one time, they believe, the continents were all part of a single continent. *Pangaea,* the super continent, broke apart and the pieces drifted slowly to their current positions. Have you ever noticed how South America and Africa look as though they are two puzzle pieces that fit together?

To add to this theory, geologists have discovered distinctive rock layers that link South America and Africa. Fossils—tracks, traces, and preserved specimens of past life—also show that either the world has greatly changed or the land has relocated. For example, fossils of mesosaurs, reptiles that lived about 200 million years ago, have been found only in South America and Africa. From the body structure of these animals, it doesn't look as if they could have survived a long swim across the ocean or even a long walk across a land bridge. So geologists believe these animals must have lived on a land area that only broke apart later, after they became extinct.

The most recent discovery, and the most convincing evidence for the theory of plate tectonics, came from Project Mohole. This was an attempt made in the 1960s to drill to the mantle in the ocean where the crust is the thinnest. The project was abandoned in 1966, but research in mapping and collecting samples from the ocean bottom revealed some surprising information. First, a mid-Atlantic rift, a large fault, was discovered running like a zipper down the middle of the Mid-Atlantic Ridge, a mountain chain stretching 10,000 miles along the length of the Atlantic ocean basin. Rock material collected close to this rift was found to be quite young. However, rock material collected close to the continents was much older. Geologists concluded that mantle material must be pouring

Aluminum Company of America

out at the rift and flowing sideways, pushing the continents apart as the seafloor spreads.

Then geologists wondered what happened to the oldest rock material. The earth, as far as anyone could tell, wasn't growing bigger. So the spreading obviously wasn't going on and on. The answer was found in the deep ocean trenches like those off the West Coast of the United States. Being closest to the continent, this would be the oldest rock material. Geologists expected such ancient rock to be covered by thick sediment. What they discovered was only a thin deposit of debris.

The conclusion was that the crustal plates are moving and interacting in response to a cycle. As *magma*, or mantle material, flows out at the rift and spreads, the plates are propelled along until they collide. Then one plate slides under another, thrusting a section of the lithosphere (the crust and half of the mantle) back

19

into the mantle before much sediment has time to accumulate. This process is called *subduction.* The interaction of the plates caused by the cycle of outflow and subduction of magma creates the tensions and pressures that shape the earth. This usually happens very slowly, but sometimes it occurs with a dramatic suddenness that makes the earth quake. Sections of plates that move together and are acted upon as a unit by these forces are referred to as *terranes.*

This diagram shows what geologists believe to be the pattern of the earth's surface plates. Arrows show the direction in which the plates are thought to be moving. Notice that the edge of a continent isn't always the edge of a plate.

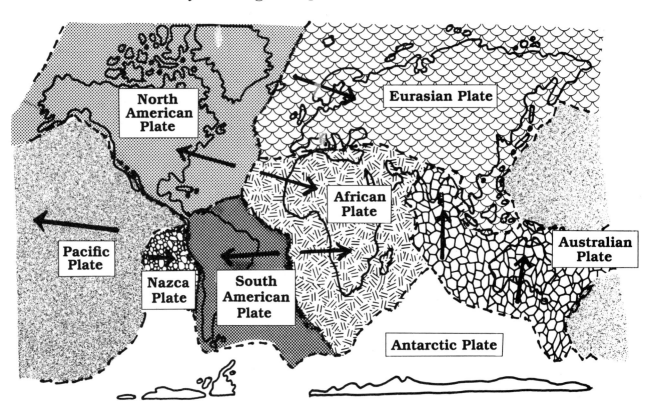

Mountain Building

More than one-fourth of the earth's land is covered by mountains. Most of these surface chains were formed as the crustal plates collided. Compression created by the plates pushing against each other over millions of years built up pressure that slowly deformed rocks. For a faster look at compression in action, lay a sheet of notebook paper flat on a desk or a tabletop. Press the palm of one hand down on each end of the sheet and begin to slide one hand toward the other very slowly. The paper will hump up into a fold. When the earth's crust crumples, *fold mountains* are formed. The Himalaya mountains were created when the plate India is riding on rammed into the Eurasian plate. In fact, this push is still going on, so the Himalayas are continuing to grow taller.

Geological Survey of Canada

The Rocky Mountains of British Columbia clearly show the folded layers of rock that formed these peaks.

Tension is another force that can change the land and construct mountains. Hold one end of a wooden pencil in each hand and slowly pull down on both ends. The pencil will bend more and more. When it suddenly snaps, a process called *elastic rebound* will make the two halves straighten. However, the jolting release of energy will make at least one of your hands jerk so that the two parts of the pencil are no longer touching. Tension builds up along faults as one chunk of the crust tries to slide past another. When one block moves vertically during elastic rebound, the fault is referred to as a *dip-slip fault* and *fault block mountains* are formed. If the movement resulting from elastic rebound is horizontal instead of vertical, the fault is called a *strike-slip fault*. Actually, both dip-slip and strike-slip movement may be involved during mountain building. The Sierra Nevada mountains in California are an example of fault block mountains.

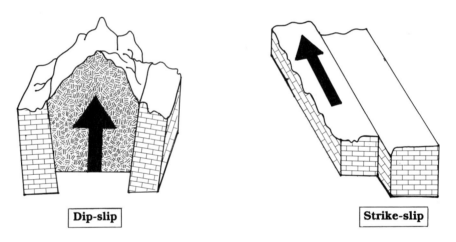

Dip-slip   Strike-slip

Probably the most famous strike-slip fault is the San Andreas in California. Along this fault, the North American plate is moving southeast while the Pacific plate is moving northwest.

Elastic rebound has caused hundreds of minor tremors and two major quakes during the fault's recorded history. The San Francisco quake in 1906 was the strongest, measuring 8.25 on the Richter scale. It caused seven hundred deaths, and the resulting fires did extensive damage. The San Fernando quake of 1971 had a magnitude of 6.5 on the Richter scale and caused sixty-five deaths and more than $500 billion in property damage.

Most faults are deep underground and covered over by layers of soil. The San Andreas Fault, though, extends to the surface, making ground movement easy to see and measure.

This fence was built in a straight line. Movement along the fault caused the split.

During subduction, the sinking lithosphere will melt, creating a pool of magma. Where pockets of magma build up, pushing up the layers of crust above them, *dome mountains* form. Slowly, the magma cools and hardens, and later the overlying layers of crust may erode away. Stone Mountain near Atlanta, Georgia, formed this way.

23

Or the magma may rise through *fissures*, narrow deep cracks. The chemical composition of the rising magma changes as it melts and combines with some of the rock material it comes in contact with. Later this intruding magma will also cool and harden.

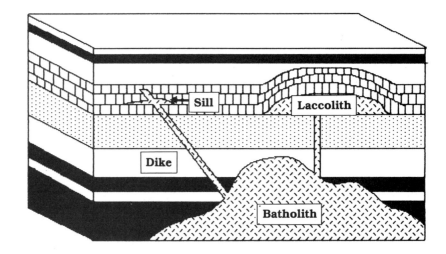

Magma that intrudes into other rock is classified by size and shape. *Dikes* are usually only a few feet thick and cut across rock layers. *Sills* are also relatively narrow but are formed when magma slips between layers of rock. *Laccoliths* form when magma pushes between rock layers but arches up the overlying layers. *Batholiths* are extremely large intrusions of magma. In fact, the mass must cover an area of more than 30 square miles to be considered a batholith. These huge intrusions often form the base of mountain ranges and are later exposed by erosion.

If magma reaches the surface, it's called *lava*. It may spread, forming broad plateaus, or it can pile up, creating a mountain. Some volcanoes are extremely fast growing and may rise to great heights within a few years. For example, Paricutín, a volcano about 200 miles west of Mexico City, began in 1943 when glowing cinders shot out of a small hole in a cornfield. The surprised farmer, Dionisio Pulido, tried to fill the hole with dirt, but this didn't stop the volcano. By the next day, the hole had turned into a *crater*— the opening at the top of a volcano—nearly 6 feet across with a lip of cinders 20 inches high. Ash and hot stones were tossed as much

Paricutín erupted steadily until March 4, 1952, when, at a height of 1,345 feet, it suddenly stopped growing.

as 15 feet into the air. Within a few days the explosions became more powerful, ejecting lava 3,000 feet into the air. A cloud of ash and smoke rose even higher as the new mountain grew to 500 feet. By the end of its first year, Paricutín had reached a height of about 1,200 feet and was more than half a mile across.

To see how a volcano erupts, you can build your own model mountain. You'll need:

a measuring cup
flour
salt
a bowl
a spoon
water
red and green food coloring
white glue
a piece of brown construction paper
a piece of poster board
scissors
a cardboard tube (from a roll of toilet paper)
a cookie sheet
baking soda
vinegar

Pour one-half cup flour and one-half cup salt into the bowl. Stir, adding cool water slowly until the mixture makes a soft but not sticky dough. Mix in just enough red and green food coloring to make the dough look brown. Glue the brown paper onto the poster board. Cut a hole about the size of a fifty-cent piece through the center of the poster board and paper. Cut off about an inch of the cardboard tube and set the tube over the hole. Then mold the dough around the tube, folding it over the top edge, and pat it into a cone-shaped volcano. Let your model mountain harden overnight.

Then place the poster board with the mountain on the cookie sheet. Scoop two tablespoons of baking soda into the *central vent*, the opening in the middle of a volcano. Drip in two drops of red food coloring and pour in two tablespoons of vinegar.

Pressures from the chemical reaction between the baking soda and the vinegar will build until the fake lava erupts. The pressure in a real volcano is created by a reaction similar to the one that happens when you uncap a bottle of soda pop. Look through the side of a bottle of pop—if possible look at a clear plastic or glass bottle. Do you see any bubbles? Take off the cap and look again. The fizz in soda comes from carbon dioxide gas. While the gas is under pressure inside the sealed bottle, it remains in solution. As soon as the pressure is released by popping the cap, the gas escapes as bubbles. Gases are held in solution in magma by the pressure of the overlying crust. When cracks in the crust release this pressure, the gas expands—sometimes explosively—forcing the magma up.

Volcanologists, people who study volcanoes, have been able to predict volcanic eruptions with increasing accuracy. One of the telltale signs they watch for is increased earthquake activity in the vicinity of the volcano. Tremors indicate that rising magma is disrupting rocks. The cracking and shifting earth creating the quake may also release pressure, causing gases in the magma to expand rapidly. Another sign is the formation of a bulge somewhere on the mountain.

On March 20, 1980, increasingly violent tremors led volcanologists to predict that magma was rising in an ancient, snow-covered volcano called Mount Saint Helens in Washington State. An immediate evacuation of the area around the mountain was ordered. It was hard for people who lived on or near the mountain—some had lived there all of their lives—to believe that this was an *active* volcano. Most left, however, and stayed away even when days passed and nothing happened. Then, on March 27, the mountain began to smoke as a crater appeared near the top. This crater enlarged, and early in April the north slope of the mountain began to swell. The world watched and waited, but surprisingly the mountain grew quiet.

Was that all? Had the volcano become inactive again? As the sun rose on May 18, 1980, the long-awaited eruption finally happened. First, an earthquake measuring 5.1 on the Richter scale shook the mountain. This was the trigger. Cracks appeared on the rocky slopes, part of the mountainside slumped, and Mount Saint Helens exploded. A thick cloud of hot ash rose 12 miles, darkening the sky. A powerful shock wave snapped whole forests of trees off at ground level. Melted ice and snow mixed with ash and hot gas, forming boiling mud that roared down the mountain's sides.

In the days that followed that major eruption, half of Spirit Lake at the base of the mountain became filled with mud. The narrow Toutle River that drains that area was transformed into a wide, surging river of mud that carried away everything in its path. The mouth of the Columbia River, into which the Toutle dumped its muddy load, became so clogged that oceangoing ships were trapped in inland harbors. The Army Corps of Engineers had to dredge a deep enough channel to restore a shipping lane. A blizzard of sharp, glassy particles of ash fell over the entire northwest. In Washington and parts of Montana and Idaho, the settling ash was as deep as a heavy snow. Only the ash didn't melt; it had to be shoveled up and hauled away.

To see your model explode the way Mount Saint Helens did, wad up a paper tissue and tuck it into the top of your volcano. Stack up two equal piles of books and place your volcano across these like a bridge. Now aim the nozzle of a blow dryer up the central vent and switch it on. Like the plug of rock and exploding magma, the tissue will swell outward until it's blasted free.

Despite the property loss and damage caused by Mount Saint

Helens' eruption, there was little loss of life because people heeded the warnings. The story was much different when the volcano Nevado del Ruiz, 85 miles northwest of Bogotá, Colombia, erupted in mid-November 1985. Almost a year earlier a series of minor earthquakes had alerted volcanologists. Even though Nevado del Ruiz is close to the equator, it is buried under glaciers, and it had been quiet since 1845. No one believed warnings that this ice-covered mountain could belch fire. About two months before the eruption, the volcano began to vent smoke and finally ash. People living below the mountain ignored even these signs of the volcano's renewed activity. Then it was too late. The eruption came out under the glacier, melting the ice and creating a mudflow that roared into the valley below the volcano. The results were devastating. Whole villages were buried, and more than 20,000 people were killed.

Hawaii Visitors Bureau

This volcanic eruption is from Kilauea Iki, a crater on the rim of the much larger Kilauea crater in Hawaii. Its most spectacular eruption was in 1959 when fountains of fire spouted 1,900 feet into the sky.

When small lava particles harden, they form ash. Chunks of frothy lava are called *pumice.* When pumice cools and hardens, it looks like a rock sponge, and the many holes make it light enough to float in water. Larger volcanic bombs may also be blown out during an eruption. Lava that runs down the sides of a volcano may be thin or fairly thick.

You can investigate what happens to flowing lava by pouring one tablespoon of molasses or pancake syrup onto a piece of waxed paper. Tip the paper slightly and watch the sticky liquid move. Let the syrup set for a couple of hours and tip the paper again. Notice whether the syrup flows faster or slower after it has set. Touch the syrup. Can you tell that it's still liquid inside the leathery skin that formed as the syrup began to harden? Prick the outer film with a toothpick, tip the paper, and watch what happens. Lava cools the same way the syrup hardens—from the outside in. Hot lava traveling through the tunnels of cooling lava pushes out the end and flows on.

When lava pours into water, it hardens very quickly. Drip a little syrup into ice water. Compare these syrup strands to those on the waxed paper. See how much faster the syrup hardens in ice water. Lava that has cooled underwater, like that in the picture, looks like large bed pillows and is called *pillow lava.* If geologists find pillow lava formations on dry land, they know that area was once under water.

Geological Survey of Canada

There are three main kinds of volcanic mountains—*shield, cinder cone*, and *composite cone.*

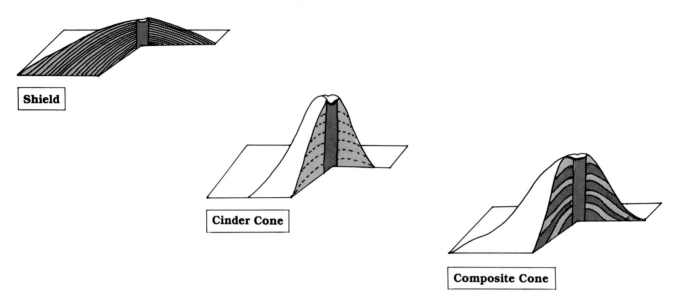

Shield volcanoes are formed by runny lava. They are often made up of thousands of layers, but each layer is thin and spread out. So the mountain takes a flattened shield shape. Mauna Loa and Mauna Kea on the island of Hawaii are shield volcanoes. Mauna Loa is the world's largest active volcano. Inactive Mauna Kea would be the world's highest mountain (33,476 feet) if measured from its base on the floor of the ocean. Cinder cone volcanoes usually have very steep sides. They form when a volcano belches only cinders and ash. Paricutín in Mexico is a cinder cone volcano. A composite cone develops when a volcano pours out lava followed by cinders and ash. Then, later, it erupts lava again. These mountains have the prettiest shapes. Mount Fuji in Japan and Mount Vesuvius in Italy are composite volcanoes.

New Land

In the cold, gray, early hours of November 14, 1963, a cod-fishing boat near the Westman Islands, off the southern coast of Iceland, suddenly twisted as if caught in a whirlpool. Then the fishermen on board noticed dark smoke rising from the sea to the south. They immediately radioed the coast guard, believing that a ship must be burning, but they were told no SOS had been received. Curious, the fishermen sailed closer.

What they saw was a new island—an erupting volcano—emerging from the sea. The ocean is nearly 425 feet deep in that location, so the volcano had already been active for a long time to reach sea level. The cloud of ash and smoke rose to 12,000 feet, and by November 16 the island was 130 feet high and 1,800 feet long. Over the next few weeks the eruption column sometimes soared to 50,000 feet as the volcano continued to build the new island. By December 30, 1963, the cone was 500 feet high and the island covered about a square mile—one-half the size of Central Park in New York City.

Surtsey, as the new island was named, didn't last. A few years later an explosive eruption made the island sink beneath the surface again. However, during its brief existence, Surtsey was a real-life laboratory for *geomorphologists,* people who study how the earth's features form. *Biologists,* people who study plant and animal life, also watched in wonder as plants and animals quickly invaded the new island. Volcanologists continue to watch this area because the volcano is still active, and there is speculation that it will one day reappear as an island. Surtsey is a reminder of the internal forces that are constantly at work building and shaping the earth's crust.

Earth Heat

Iceland, an island about half the size of Kansas in the far, cold reaches of the North Atlantic, has learned how to take advantage of its unusual natural resource—active volcanoes. Iceland straddles the Mid-Atlantic Ridge, and like its temporary neighbor, Surtsey, it can trace its origin to magma pouring out of the rift far below on the ocean bottom. Over the centuries, eruptions have claimed lives and destroyed property. However, the underground molten material has also heated the groundwater. This is known as *geothermal,* meaning literally "earth heat," heat. As early as the 1930s, Icelanders discovered the value of using this naturally hot water. Today, between 65 and 70 percent of all buildings in Iceland—and all of the buildings in Reykjavík, the capital—use this inexpensive, pollution-free source of heat and hot water. Even though Reykjavík's main supply is pumped from 10 miles away, the water channeled through concrete-covered pipes is still 165 to 175° F when it reaches the city. Greenhouses heated with geo-thermal heat supply Iceland with fresh fruits and vegetables during the long, cold winter months.

Mountain Match

The list on the left shows the highest mountain on each continent. Can you match the mountain to the continent it's on? The answers appear upside down at the bottom.

1.	Aconcagua (22,835 feet)	A.	Australia
2.	Elbrus (18,481 feet)	B.	North America
3.	Everest (29,028 feet)	C.	Antarctica
4.	Kilimanjaro (19,340 feet)	D.	Europe
5.	Kosciusko (7,316 feet)	E.	Asia
6.	McKinley (20,320 feet)	F.	Africa
7.	Vinson Massif (16,860 feet)	G.	South America

Did you know that you can see all fifty of the highest mountains in the United States by visiting just four states—Alaska, California, Colorado, and Washington?

Even as the forces shaping the earth are building up mountains over millions of years, other forces are at work tearing them down. Mountains that are high with sharp, rocky peaks like the Purcell range in British Columbia, Canada, are young mountains. Other, rounded, tree-covered mountains, such as the Great Smokies in North Carolina, have been under attack for a very long time. What forces can destroy mountains? That's what you'll explore in the next chapter.

Answers: 1.G, 2.D, 3.E, 4.F, 5.A, 6.B, 7.C

This is a picture of the Grand Canyon in Arizona. According to Indian lore, it was formed when a god struck the earth with an axe. A story about Paul Bunyan, the giant lumberjack, explains that he created it by carelessly dragging a huge peavey, a hook for moving logs. These make good tall tales, but the Grand Canyon wasn't carved by an Indian god or a giant.

Investigating Forces That Break Down and Move

National Park Service

How Was the Grand Canyon Carved?

A river did it. About ten million years ago, the forces that shape and build the earth uplifted the area drained by what was much later named the Colorado River. Then, what had been a slow, meandering waterway became a fast-swirling, turbulent river, rushing down to the Gulf of Mexico.

To see how this is possible, line a 9×13 inch metal cake pan or a shallow cardboard box with a plastic garbage bag and pack it full of soil. Let the soil sit outdoors in a sunny spot until it's dry and hard. Next, put the pan or box in an open area and spray it with a garden hose turned on full force. What happens to the soil?

Look at the picture of the Grand Canyon again. In this dry, barren environment the earth was exposed and unprotected. Wind, the pull of gravity, plants, and animals helped break rock material loose and carry it away. Splashing raindrops and moisture seeping into cracks in rocks and expanding as it froze attacked the land too. However, it was always the river that was the most powerful carving force. Particle by particle the Colorado River pried rock fragments free. Then these chips and chunks became abrasive tools that knocked even more rock grains loose. The Spaniards named the river Colorado, meaning "red colored," because the water was so thick with sediment.

Before the Glen Canyon Dam was built, the river carried 500,000 tons of sand, silt (rock particles of an intermediate size between sand and clay), and mud through the Grand Canyon gorge every day. That's enough solid material to fill two million quarter-ton pickup trucks. No wonder people said the Colorado River was "too thin to plow but too thick to drink." Over millions of years, the river had ground its bed down more than 5,000 feet into the earth. Today the Colorado River continues to dig deeper but more slowly. This decreased pace is partly because it has reached a particularly resistant rock layer called Vishnu schist and partly because the Glen Canyon Dam controls the amount of water flowing through the gorge. Less water means less cutting force.

The Grand Canyon today has many visitors but it was mysterious and unmapped until Major John Wesley Powell and a crew of nine men set out to explore it. They started downriver on May 24,

1869, in four small wooden boats. It was a terrible journey. Each new bend in the river brought new risks and hardships. Three men quit and climbed out of the canyon. The remaining men struggled on for nearly three months. Growing weary, their food running out, they began to wonder if they would ever escape. Daily, the cliffs seemed to stretch higher above their heads. Finally, on August 30, 1869, Powell and his five remaining crewmen glided out of the gorge. They had successfully mapped the Grand Canyon.

To find out more about this exciting true-adventure story, look for a biography of Major John Wesley Powell at your local library.

Break It Down

Weathering is the process through which the earth's destructive forces break up rocks. There are two main kinds of weathering—*mechanical* and *chemical*.

During mechanical weathering, also called disintegration, rocks are broken down into smaller pieces, but even the tiniest remaining piece has all the characteristics of the original. The basic molecular structure is not altered. The way the molecules are grouped determines the kind of matter that is formed, such as salt or gold. How the molecules are spaced determines the matter's state—solid, liquid, or gas.

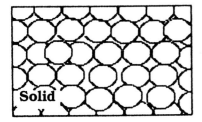
Solid

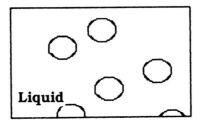
Liquid

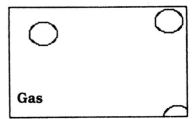
Gas

You can mechanically weather a sheet of notebook paper. Try tearing it, cutting it, folding it, crumpling it, stomping on it, and poking holes in it. The end result will look different, but you'll still be able to tell it's notebook paper. You've changed its physical properties without affecting its chemical structure.

The Grand Canyon is proof that water is one of the tools nature uses to mechanically weather rock material. Wherever a little bit

This used to be the bottom of a stream in the Paria River Canyon in Utah. When the stream dried up, the mud cracked.

of water seeps into a crack, it acts like a crowbar when it freezes, prying the rock particles apart. Normally, molecules move closer together when heat is removed, but water is different. Fill a plastic or a paper cup nearly full of water. Set the cup inside the freezer section of your refrigerator and then pour in enough additional water to fill it to the very brim. Stretch a piece of clear wrap over the top, holding it in place with a rubber band. Then close the freezer and let the cup sit overnight. When you check the next morning, you'll discover the ice poking out the top. What happened to the clear wrap as the water expanded? Frozen water expands 9 percent beyond its original volume, and this swelling can exert as much as 30,000 pounds of pressure per square inch.

Thermal expansion may make the initial rock cracks that the water is able to enter. Put a clear, uncracked glass marble into the freezer and leave it overnight. Before you take the marble out, start some water boiling in a saucepan on the stove or in an electric skillet. Use a wooden spoon (or a metal spoon held with a pot holder) to gently drop the marble into the boiling water. After two minutes, turn off the heat and use the spoon to fish out the marble. Surprise! The marble is covered with tiny cracks. The dramatic temperature change made the marble's molecules expand suddenly. Thermal expansion is particularly effective in desert areas like the Grand Canyon region. Without enough moisture to produce clouds, the earth isn't shielded from the sun's rays during the day so temperatures soar. At night the earth's heat isn't held in by clouds so it's quickly radiated away. Temperatures may drop more than fifty degrees once the sun sets. Look for evidence of thermal expansion going on in your community. Can you find a

36

cracked sidewalk, driveway, or wall? Tar strips are often placed between slabs of concrete. How could this help prevent thermal expansion from cracking the concrete?

Drying out, or *desiccation,* can also cause mechanical weathering. Cut the top off a plastic milk jug and use this container to mix about two cups of soil with enough water to make a thick mud. Spread the mud in the bottom of a shallow box. Then place the box outside in a sunny spot. Check the mud every day to observe how it changes as it dries out.

Another process, called *sheeting,* is similar to what happens to the nap of a carpet after a piece of heavy furniture has been moved. Freed from the pressing weight, the carpet fibers slowly spring back. Unloading—removing overlying pressure—can be enough to make rocks break. At Half Dome in Yosemite National Park, cracks developed parallel to the earth's surface and the outer layers peeled off like the layers of an onion. Stone Mountain near Atlanta, Georgia, is another mountain that was shaped by sheeting. In some deep mines, the release of overlying pressure has made rocks explode off the walls. Because they're now aware of the effects of unloading, mining engineers plan for it as they direct the construction of mine shafts.

Wind is another tool nature uses to mechanically weather rocks. Wind-driven sand and grit blast rock particles loose. Since the sand blows along the ground, wind-eroded rocks like the ones pictured below are skinnier at the bottom than they are at the top. Wind erosion can scour off paint, pit glass, and cut through telephone poles in time. Can you find any examples of wind erosion in your neighborhood?

You can see these wind-carved, odd-looking sculptures at the Arches National Monument in Utah.

Ward's Natural Science Establishment, Inc.

Burrowing animals may weather rocks as they dig, and plant roots may push into cracks, helping to pry particles apart. Have you ever seen a cracked, pushed-up sidewalk with tree roots poking through the concrete?

People also weather rocks as they dig tunnels, level land, and blast open cuts for roads. Highway engineers have to consider how exposed rock surfaces will weather. Where Highway I-40 was cut through the Great Smoky Mountains between Asheville, North Carolina, and Knoxville, Tennessee, the rocks crumbled rapidly. At one time the only protection drivers had between themselves and the falling rocks was a barrier of junk cars—hundreds of cars, smashed flat and stacked three deep. In 1982 a chunk of rock 200 feet wide crashed onto the road, temporarily closing it. After several people were killed by falling rocks, a $13-million project was launched to try to slow down the mechanical weathering process. Holes were drilled through any questionable rock to the solid rock beneath. Then epoxy glue was added, and a steel bolt about an inch wide and as much as 90 feet long was shoved into the hole. Finally, a hydraulic jack applied 70,000 pounds of pressure to the bolt, and a giant nut anchored it in place.

In a similar attempt to slow down the mechanical weathering that is destroying the nearly perfect conical shape of Mount Fuji, an inactive volcano in Japan, a massive concrete wall was built across a widening chasm. This mountain Band-Aid was 10 feet thick, 16 feet high, and 55 feet long. As much as 300,000 tons of soil and rock had been tumbling away every year.

Sometimes people cause creative weathering. Stone Mountain near Atlanta, Georgia, is a monumental example. In 1915 the United Daughters of the Confederacy leased the mountain and planned to have Robert E. Lee's image etched on the bare granite. However, efforts to make the memorial were slowed by disagreements and changes of both artist and design. The plan expanded to include figures of Jefferson Davis and Thomas "Stonewall" Jackson on horseback with Lee. The carving proceeded slowly because large areas couldn't be removed with explosives. The blast would have caused huge cracks to form in the granite mountain. Then the lease expired. Work didn't begin again until 1958—after a thirty-year delay—when the state decided to develop the mountain as a tourist attraction.

This time a new tool, the thermo-jet torch, was used. Burning as hot as 4,000° F, the torch could peel off several tons of stone a day. The stone carvers worked year round—in intense heat and chilling cold. Finally, in March 1972, the carving was completed. The three figures together are 90 feet tall and 190 feet long. Traveller, Lee's horse, alone is 145 feet long with relief carving so deep that there's room for a car to drive along his back.

The memorial at Stone Mountain is impressive, but just because it's carved out of stone doesn't mean it will last forever. Have you ever seen a stone tombstone with its message nearly weathered away? At Mount Rushmore National Memorial in South Dakota, workers annually patch the sculptured heads of George Washington, Thomas Jefferson, Theodore Roosevelt, and Abraham Lincoln to keep these stony faces from cracking up. They also mow the weeds that sprout on Jefferson's cheeks. Because plants produce a tiny amount of acid at their root tips to help them break up rock particles, this weedy beard would gradually weather the rock enough to create a thin layer of soil and change Jefferson's complexion.

Lichens are plants that are particularly good at weathering rocks. Have you ever seen a flat, crusty-looking plant growing on bare rocks? Lichens are a partnership between a fungus and an alga. The fungal cells produce an acid that breaks up the surface of the rock. The algal cells use minerals freed by this process to produce food. Find a place where lichens are growing on a rock and carefully pry one plant away. Underneath, you'll find tiny, crumbled rock particles.

Chemical weathering, also called decomposition, occurs when air, water, and the substances dissolved in water change the molecular structure of the elements in rocks. Sometimes the openings in rocks that let in moisture and air are too small to be seen easily. Weigh a small piece of brick on a kitchen scale and write down the results. Then put the brick into a bowl, completely cover it with water, and let it sit overnight. The next day, weigh the brick again. It will be heavier. How much heavier is it? Why do you think the rock gained weight?

The climate has a big influence on how much chemical weathering affects rocks. Heat speeds up molecular activity. So warm, moist environments, such as tropical rain forests and much of the United States during the summer, have conditions that are perfect for decomposition of rocks. Rock masses in dry, cold places, such as areas north of the Arctic Circle, are not affected very much by chemical weathering.

Rocks containing iron-magnesium minerals decompose easily. The iron combines with oxygen to form rust. Georgia's red clay is a result of the chemical weathering of iron-magnesium minerals. The Redwall limestone layer of the Grand Canyon is naturally gray, but red iron oxides washing down from layers higher up have stained it.

Place an unrusty iron nail in a glass jar, seal the opening tightly with a lid or clear wrap, and put the jar into the freezer. Place another unrusty iron nail in a glass jar full of water and let it sit uncovered in a warm spot. Check both nails every day. Add more water as needed to keep the nail in the open jar covered. Which nail is the first to show signs of rusting? Continue to make daily observations for at least a week. What if both nails were exposed to the air and water? Would the cold nail still be slower to rust?

Some rocks, such as halite, or rock salt, will dissolve in water. Put two tablespoons of salt into a glass of water and stir. Eventually you won't be able to see the granular salt particles. Limestone, a rock formed most often by the shells of sea animals settling to the bottom and becoming compacted by overlying layers, can be easily dissolved by a weak acid. Drip a few drops of vinegar onto a piece of limestone. If you don't have any limestone in your area, try the same test on a little pile of broken seashells. Or drip a little vinegar onto some broken pieces of chalk. As long as you use real chalk and not a synthetic variety, it will react like limestone because chalk is also made up of tiny, compressed seashells. As soon as the vinegar touches the limestone, bubbles will form. Rub your finger in the foam. Do you feel the tiny, gritty particles of dissolved rock?

Water picks up carbon dioxide from the air and from the soil, forming a weak acid called *carbonic acid.* This reacts with limestone, dissolving it the way the vinegar did. Limestones readily weather, and the dissolved material may seep away, leaving a hollowed-out place in the earth. Pile up a wall of sugar cubes in a glass pie plate or baking dish to represent a limestone formation. Mix two drops of food coloring into a cup of water and spoon 10 teaspoons of colored water—one at a time—onto the top cubes. Observe after each teaspoon is poured on. How many teaspoons does it take before the water soaks through to the bottom? How many teaspoons did you add before chemical weathering first began to dissolve the sugar?

Notice the depression that forms after all 10 teaspoons of water have been poured on. If it had a ceiling, this hollowed-out area would be a cave or a cavern (a very large cave). Touch the liquid in the bottom of the dish. It's sticky. After water causes chemical weathering, it carries the dissolved minerals away. Later, if the roof of the cave collapses, a sinkhole forms. This may happen slowly or suddenly. If part of the cave roof remains, it appears as a natural bridge.

That Sinking Feeling

At 8 P.M. on Friday, May 8, 1981, Mrs. Mae Rose Owen of Winter Park, Florida, suddenly noticed that a giant sycamore tree was sinking in her front yard. When it had completely disappeared, she rushed to call the police. Mrs. Owen's tree was only the beginning. Rainwater seeping into cracks and crevices had, over millions of years, dissolved the limestone bedrock beneath Winter Park. As long as the cavern created by the removal of this material remained flooded, the surface topsoil continued to be supported. However, demands for water by the growing residential and industrial community plus a lengthy drought lowered the water level in the cavern dramatically. Finally, the ceiling collapsed. It was as if the plug in a tub had been pulled. After Mrs. Owen's tree, the deep end of the Westside Municipal Pool went, along with a whole section of street, houses, trees, utility poles, and cars. Then even more of Winter Park disappeared. Eventually the sinkhole spread to a width of more than 400 feet and a depth of 150 feet.

Today the sinkhole has stopped growing and filled with water. Winter Park now has a pretty little lake right in the middle of town. Although this formation was more dramatic than most, this is the way many of Florida's small lakes have formed.

National Park Service

Spelunkers are people who explore caves. If you went spelunking in this cavern, you'd be in one of the biggest in the United States. Carlsbad Caverns in New Mexico has rooms that extend for more than 15 miles. One very big room is about 4,000 feet long and more than 600 feet wide—big enough to hold twenty baseball fields. The ceiling of that room is more than 300 feet high.

Drop-by-Drop Rocks

When a cave is no longer flooded, water seeping down through overlying layers of limestone may begin to deposit new rocks. Pour one cup of water into a saucepan and heat until it's hot but not boiling. Immediately stir in two-thirds cup of Epsom salts (inexpensive and available at your local grocery store). When the salt crystals have completely dissolved, divide the solution equally between two small juice glasses. Set both glasses in a glass baking dish, placing them about 3 inches apart. Wet a piece of yarn by submerging it in one glass. Squeeze out any extra liquid. Then string the yarn between the two glasses, dipping one end into the liquid in each glass. If the ends float to the surface, tie them to paper clips. As you watch, a drop will form at the center of the string and drip off, leaving a little bit of salt behind. In a cave, as each drip forms, evaporation takes place, depositing a film of calcium carbonate. These drops gradually build a stalactite, resembling a rock icicle. Stalactites may create fanciful shapes and even be beautifully colored by residues of other minerals. No two stalactites are alike. Stalagmites may also build up where the drops—still carrying a trace of calcium carbonate—land on the cave floor. You'll be able to remember which type of formation hangs from the ceiling. It's the one with a *c* in the middle. Stalagmites with a *g* build up from the ground. Columns are formed when stalactites and stalagmites join. After an hour remove the glasses and allow the liquid in the glass dish to sit overnight. The next morning hold the dish up to the light to view the frostlike crystals that formed as the water evaporated.

Earth Carvers from Space

Meteorites are rocks—space debris—that have plummeted through the earth's atmosphere and crashed into the surface. The friction of falling through the atmosphere leaves the outside of these rocks charred—even melted looking. Some meteorites are stony. Others are made up of the minerals iron and nickel. Stony meteorites often explode, showering the surface with fragments. Metallic meteorites are heavy and if large may smack into the earth with enough force to create a crater. The largest and most impressive spot on the earth's crust shaped by a chunk of falling space debris is the crater at Canyon Diablo near Winslow, Arizona. This bowl-shaped hole is 4,000 feet across and 570 feet deep. Many tiny pieces of metallic meteorite have been discovered around the crater. Geologists believe impact was about 75,000 years ago.

Take It Away

Erosion is the movement of weathered material, and sometimes gravity's pull is all that's needed. Rubble that tumbles down to pile up at the base of a mountain, as in the picture below, forms what is called a *talus cone*.

Ward's Natural Science Establishment, Inc.

If a large mass of rock breaks loose and slides downhill, the result is a *rockslide*. Earthquakes can trigger rockslides. Or heavy rains may loosen underlying material. A rockslide can be extremely destructive, smashing through forests, houses—anything in its path. In fairly dry areas, slopes are often covered with loose, unprotected soil. There, sudden heavy rains can transform the bare soil into mud. The *mudflow* that resulted from the 1985 eruption of the Nevado del Ruiz volcano near Bogotá, Colombia, buried whole villages. Mudflows have also periodically damaged large numbers of houses in California. Those homes were built in canyons—despite deposits that were a geologic record of mudflows that had poured through that area in the past. *Creep* is a much slower downslope movement that happens when the ground repeatedly cycles through periods of being wet and then dry or of freezing and then thawing.

The Colorado River is proof that not only does water weather rock, it carries loose material away. How much is moved and how far it goes depends on the amount of water, how fast the water is flowing, and whether the ground has a protective covering of vegetation. Even a single raindrop can cause *splash erosion*. You can demonstrate what happens to the earth when a raindrop strikes by throwing a rubber ball into a mud puddle. Raindrops bombard bare soil like little bombs. The water's natural surface tension, the tendency of water molecules to stick together, also quickly seals the ground, preventing water from soaking in. This increases the runoff that carries away loose soil and rock particles.

How effective is ground cover in protecting the soil? Use electrician's tape to attach five white 5×7 index cards to Popsicle sticks. Choose five different places to push these sticks into the earth so that the bottom edge of the card is at ground level. At least one card should be in bare soil, and one should be in a grass-covered area. Try to find areas with varying degrees of ground cover for the other cards. Check after a rain. Which cards are mud-splattered, showing that the

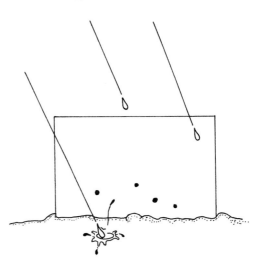

raindrops knocked soil loose? If you live in a city, go looking for places that are soil-stained because of splash erosion. Take along a tape measure and measure how high up the soil has splashed in each case. What do you think could be done to help stop splash erosion?

Since individual raindrops have enough force to move soil particles, think what a fast-flowing river can do. To simulate how uplift affected the Colorado River's eroding power, try this investigation. Smooth out the surface of your pan or box full of soil again. Then, with an old spoon, dig a shallow channel straight from one side to the other. Prop up one end of the pan as shown and place the other end in a jellyroll pan or a larger, plastic-lined box to catch any overflowing water. You may want to have a friend pour one cup of water into your river channel at the upper end while you hold a glass jar to collect the discharge. Use a crayon to mark the water level on the outside of the jar. Let the water you collect sit for several hours.

How much sediment settled to the bottom of the jar—a lot or only a little? Rinse out your collection jar. Then repeat the test, keeping all the conditions the same except elevation. Tip the river channel much more steeply. Mark the new water level with a different-colored crayon and let the jar sit. Was there more or less discharge this time? Does the faster-flowing water cause more or less sediment to settle out? More sediment means more abrasive action along the bottom of the streambed.

To investigate how the amount of water flowing through the stream affects erosion, keep the elevation steep and pour four cups of water—one after the other—into the mouth of the channel. You may first need to repair your channel if too much erosion has occurred in earlier experiments. Compare the amount of discharge and the amount of sediment to that collected when the stream flow was only one cup of water.

Finally, bury a large rock beneath your stream channel and pour on enough water to erode down to the rock. Then pour on two more cups of water. What happens? Rapids or waterfalls may form. Niagara Falls—shared by the United States and Canada—was formed when the Niagara River eroded down to an 80-foot-thick layer of dolomite, a resistant type of rock, overlying less resistant material. This rock didn't line the entire bed. Beyond it, the river was able to carve easily through soft layers of limestone, sandstone, and shale. A cliff in a river creates a waterfall. So the point where the dolomite cap ended quickly became Niagara Falls.

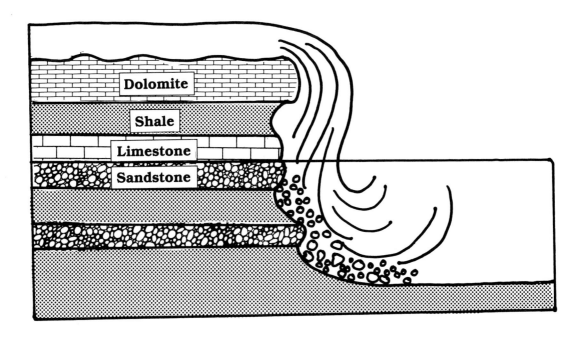

Over many years, the falls have slowly backed up about 7 miles as the churning river splashes back, undercutting the cap. Bit by bit, unsupported chunks of dolomite have broken away. Niagara Falls is really two falls, Horseshoe Falls and the American Falls, separated by a small island. Horseshoe Falls is eroding much faster—nearly 3 feet each year compared to only 4 to 6 inches per year at the American Falls—because 90 percent of the water pours over this section. When the cap is gone, the river will quickly cut its bed down to the level of the rest of the gorge.

In the 1960s residents in communities near the falls became concerned about the crumbling dolomite. Niagara Falls is important both because it attracts tourists and because it supplies hydroelectric power. In 1969 the Army Corps of Engineers was called in to try to stop the erosion that is slowly destroying the falls. First a dam was built to temporarily shut off the American Falls. Then workers cemented over the eroding areas. Plans were discussed for a major overhaul of Horseshoe Falls, but the estimated costs and the effort required were too great.

So don't wait too long if you plan to visit this famous falls. At its current erosion rate, geologists estimate that the Niagara River will probably only continue to fall for another 22,800 years.

Where Does the Eroded Material Go?

In the aerial view shown on the next page, the Hay River in Alberta, Canada, twists snakelike because of *meanders*—bends in the channel. No one is quite sure why meanders start—possibly because the river encounters an obstacle as it cuts into its bed and follows the course of least resistance. However, once meanders begin, sediment cut away from the outside of the riverbank is deposited on the inside of the meander. By cutting and depositing, the river very, very slowly slithers across the land. If two meanders happen to run into each other, a *cutoff* forms, connecting the two loops at the top. Then the river flows through the cutoff because that's the shortest route. The abandoned meander becomes an *oxbow lake*. Gradually it fills with sediment, forming a *meander scar.*

Look closely at this aerial view of the Hay River in northern Alberta, Canada. Can you find a meander with a cutoff? Can you spot an oxbow lake?

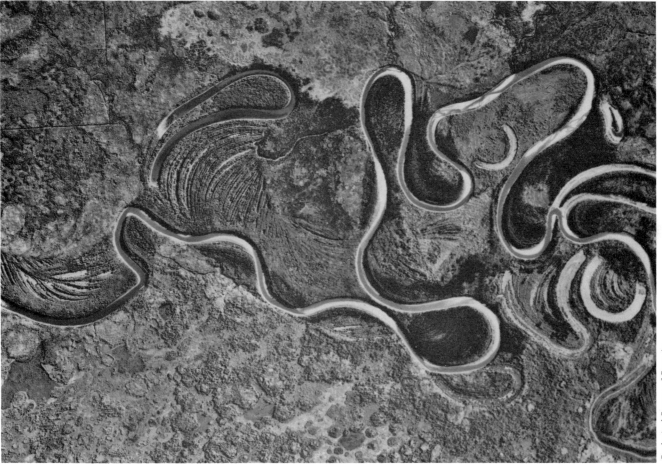

Geological Survey of Canada

Even if meanders don't form, the rock particles being swept along are deposited as the water slows so much that it can't hold the material in suspension. That's why sediment piles up on the inside bank of a meander. Water moves more slowly on this side of the river bend. If the channel's elevation suddenly becomes less steep, deposits are dropped, building up a fan. This often happens at the base of a mountain. When rivers flow into the ocean, sediment is dumped in the calm water. There the often broad deposit that builds up at the mouth of a river is called a *delta*. Thirty-one of the forty-eight contiguous United States have rivers that eventually drain into the Mississippi River system. So it's no wonder that this mighty river dumps an average of a million tons of sediment a day into the Gulf of Mexico. The Mississippi River delta has built up land covering approximately 12,000 square miles.

Mix up a jar of "river soup" to see what happens when fast-moving water slows down. Fill a quart jar half full of water. Dump in a handful of pebbles, one-quarter cup of sand, and one-quarter cup of soil. Pour in enough water to nearly fill the jar, stir well, and let the mixture sit for several hours. Draw and color a picture of the layers that form. Take a close look through the glass. The heaviest material settled first. What is on the bottom? What is on the top?

Hold That River

A river that is rearranging its meanders and depositing sediment to build up land at its mouth can cause problems. A farmer would rather not have the bank of his side of the river carried away and added onto his neighbor's land. Merchants and shipping companies need deep channels for freighters to navigate. Nobody wants muddy river water sloshing through homes and businesses when the river floods. Worldwide, floods cause more damage to property—nearly a billion dollars a year in the United States—and more loss of life than any other national disaster. Historically, the most deadly flood was when China's Yellow River overflowed in 1887, killing 9 million people. One of the most famous floods in the United States happened in 1889 when the Conemaugh River flooded Johnstown, Pennsylvania, killing 2,200 people. When the Mississippi River flooded in 1927, water spread over 80 miles from the main channel. Two hundred million dollars' worth of property was destroyed and nearly 500 people died. After that flood, Congress funded the U.S. Army Corps of Engineers in a vast river-taming project.

A great deal of effort and many millions of dollars continues to be spent annually to try to control rivers in the United States. *Levees*—earthen embankments—are built to hold rivers in their banks. *Jetties*—walls projecting into the water—are built to catch and trap sediment. Along the Mississippi this helps keep the main channel clear for shipping. *Revetments*—concrete slabs strung together on a grid of steel wires—are used to cover the outside bank of a river, protecting it from erosion. Dams are built to slow down rushing floodwaters, providing reservoirs as holding tanks for excess runoff. This has been particularly helpful where snowmelts tend to create annual spring floods. From February to October, the main shipping season, dredges work the Mississippi making sure the channel is deep and clear enough for big ships. Dredging is a constant task at New Orleans, the United States' second busiest port after New York.

In the 1930s and 1940s the U.S. Army Corps of Engineers dug a number of cutoffs across the tops of meanders to straighten out rivers. Rather than helping, this often created new problems. The "shortened" river flowed faster, picking up a bigger sediment load, which it dumped downstream. Clogged channels were more likely to flood. Recently these rivers have been carefully rerouted to their original channels in a number of places.

Pour On the Topsoil

For many hundreds of years people living along the Nile in Egypt welcomed this river's annual flood. The muddy water spread fresh deposits of rich soil on fields just in time for planting. However, after the construction of the Aswan Dam, the river no longer flooded. Lake Nasser, the reservoir behind the Aswan High Dam, covers 2,000 square miles and is the third largest man-made lake in the world. That's where the Nile pours its excess water every spring— and where it drops its load of sediment. Although farmers no longer receive the river's gift of fertile topsoil, the dam has made water available for irrigation throughout the hot, dry summer. This has increased the cultivatable land in the United Arab Republic by about one third. The dam has also greatly improved the country's economy and revolutionized its industrial abilities by making it possible to harness the Nile to generate hydroelectric power.

Investigating Soils

The ultimate product formed by rocks breaking down is soil. This picture shows a profile of good soil. Each layer is called a horizon. At the very bottom, you can see the *bedrock*. It gradually grades into crumbled rock and then *subsoil*. This transitional layer is important because water that has seeped down from above and that plants will need to grow collects here. Then comes *topsoil*. This forms as the solid rock particles mix with *humus*, decaying plant and animal matter. Scientists estimate that from 250 to 1,000 years are needed for just over 7 inches of topsoil to build up.

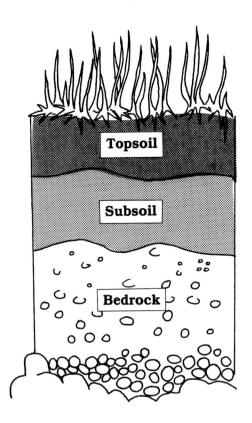

Not all soils are the same. There are as many as 70,000 varieties of soil in the United States alone, and some of these are much better than others at retaining water and supplying the essential elements plants need to grow. *Pedologists*, people who study soils, check for five physical characteristics: texture, structure, porosity, color, and chemical composition. When they know those soil traits, they can help a farmer plan what crops to raise and how to get the best yield possible. They can also advise the civil engineers who design highways, tunnels, and so forth if the soil will make a good road base or a sound bridge foundation.

Before you can start investigating soils, you'll need to go on a soil hunt. Take along several large-sized, self-sealing plastic bags, a one-cup measure, a small notepad, and a pencil. Collect soil from at least three places. For the most interesting results, make these three very different locations, such as a bare field, a flower bed, and the bank of a creek. If you live in the city, you could purchase potting soil or collect soil from a park and a construction site. Just be sure you get permission before you start digging. Scoop three cups of soil into a bag at each site. Pick out any large stones or twigs. Then make a note about where the soil was collected and what kinds of plants, if any, you see in that area. Tuck this note into the bag before sealing it. Once back home, you can compare these samples as you discover each soil's special traits.

Texture is determined by particle size. First put a pinch of each soil on a piece of white paper. Examine the particles with a magnifying glass and rub some between your fingers. Which feels grittier? Which has the largest particles? Which has more angular, sharp-edged particles? Make a note of your observations. Next, do a settling test to see how much of the soil is made up of sand, silt, and clay particles.

You'll need one large-mouthed pint jar for each sample. Tape on an identification label. Then pour in one cup of soil, add enough water to almost fill the jar, and stir. Let the particles settle until the water above the soil is nearly clear. Sand and any pebbles will be on the bottom. Silt will form the middle layer, and tiny clay grains will appear on top. Humus will probably remain floating in the water. To record the results, fold a piece of typing paper lengthwise, forming a column for each sample. Label the columns. Choose a crayon or colored pencil to represent each type of particle—sand, silt, and clay. Then, one sample at a time, hold a ruler against the jar and measure the thickness of each layer. Color a layer of the same thickness on the column for that sample.

Soil that is mostly sand is likely to let water run through so quickly that plants will dry out and die. Soil that is mostly clay may become so hard that water will run off rather than soak in. Plant roots will also have trouble penetrating it. *Loam* is the name given to an ideal mixture of clay, silt, sand, and humus. It is considered the best for plant growth.

Structure refers to the way the soil particles are arranged. Put a tablespoon of each sample on a piece of waxed paper. Examine the scoop of soil with a magnifying glass. Are the particles definitely separate—granular—or do they clump together? Record your observations above the column you colored for each sample. The texture and the structure of the soil will determine its porosity, or amount of spaces. A soil that is favorable for plant growth needs to be porous enough to let air and water easily reach the roots. However, it must not be so porous that water quickly drains away.

To check the soil's porosity, you'll need the top of a one- or two-liter plastic soft drink bottle cut off as shown in the picture at left to form a funnel, a piece of muslin (or any 100-percent-cotton cloth), a rubber band, and a wide-mouthed quart jar for each sample. Put the cloth over the funnel's neck, anchoring it in place with the rubber band. Then set the cutoff bottle in the quart jar.

Scoop one cup of soil into the funnel and slowly pour in one-half cup of water. As soon as water stops draining from the soil, pour what was collected in the jar back into the measuring cup. If the soil is very porous, most of the water will have slipped through. How much of the half-cup of water did you collect from each sample? Record that amount on the soil information chart, telling whether

54

you think that soil is very, somewhat, or only slightly porous. Why do you think farmers plow before they plant?

Color is a clue to what elements the soil contains and how much humus is present. For example, yellow, brown-orange, and red soil contain a lot of iron. Very pale soil probably contains only a little humus, whereas dark-brown and black soil often—though not always—has a lot of humus. Fertilizers are added to soils to make up for deficiencies. Visit a store that sells plant fertilizers (grocery stores often carry fertilizers for house plants) and check what minerals these contain. Plants particularly need nitrogen for healthy leaves and stems, phosphorus for seed development, and potassium for strong stems. Pedologists use a computer to analyze soil test results and report exactly how much, if any, of each of these elements must be added to improve productivity. Homeowners are given the amount to add per 100 or per 1,000 square feet. Farmers are told how many pounds to add per acre.

Whether or not a soil is acidic (contains acids formed by water mixing with the carbon dioxide from the air and humus) or alkaline (contains bases—mineral salts that can neutralize acids) is another important part of the soil's chemical composition. Some plants, such as cotton, will grow well in acidic soil—in fact, they need a certain acidity level. Grasses grow best in alkaline soil. Others, such as cherry trees, need neutral soil. To find out if your soils are acidic, alkaline, or neutral, you'll need one piece of pink and one piece of blue litmus paper per sample. (These are available at a hobby store.) Put one of each in the bottom of a clear glass or plastic cup. Cover with two tablespoons of soil and drip water on it a quarter-teaspoon at a time, until you can see the moisture reach the litmus paper. Then look through the bottom of the glass to check the color of the strips.

Litmus paper is treated with a special indicator that changes color in response to acids or bases. Pink litmus paper stays pink in an acid and turns blue in a base. Blue litmus paper turns pink in an acid and stays blue in a base. If the blue litmus paper turns pink and the pink litmus remains unchanged, the soil is acid. If the pink litmus paper turns blue and the blue litmus remains unchanged, the soil is alkaline. If neither change, the soil is neutral.

Above each column, list whether the soil sample is acid, base, or neutral.

Crushed limestone is added to soil to reduce its acidity and improve its structure. Alkaline soils usually develop because of desert or semidesert conditions. Irrigation with proper drainage can reduce the level of salts that are making the soil alkaline.

Now that you've compared the physical traits of your soil samples, which do you think would be best for growing plants? To test your prediction, you'll need the following equipment for each sample: a plastic foam cup with several small drainage holes in the bottom and three bean seeds (use dry soup beans, which are available at the grocery store). You'll also need three paper towels and a 9 × 13 inch metal cake pan. Soak the bean seeds in water overnight so they'll sprout faster. Next, fill each cup about two-thirds full of soil and label the cup to identify the sample. Then plant three seeds just below the surface in each cup. As a control—a means of comparison—wet the towels, squeeze out any excess water, and place three seeds on the moist paper. Sprinkle one-half teaspoon of water on each cup. Place the cups and the wet towels with the seeds in the cake pan and put it in a warm, sunny spot.

Check the pan every day. Every other day sprinkle on another half-teaspoon of water and remoisten the towels if they feel dry. Which seed sprouts first? Measure the growing plants every day for a week. Which plants grow the biggest? What did your control show about the importance of soil to plant growth? Record the height of the tallest plant for each soil sample. Which soil proved to be the best for growing plants? How do you think you could help plants grow equally well in the other soil samples?

Cold, Cold Ground

In far northern regions, such as parts of Alaska, it's so cold that most of the soil horizons remain frozen year round. Here, a special kind of soil called *tundra* develops. The topsoil is black with slowly decaying humus. In the summer the land is dotted with puddles because water quickly saturates the upper layer and can't sink into the frozen subsoil. During the long winter months ice crystals form, prying apart soil particles. Tundra appears to be covered with grass, but some of the low plants are actually trees, dwarfed by the harsh growing conditions.

The Land That Blew Away

U.S. Department of Agriculture

During World War I farmers in the Midwest cleared millions of acres of grassland, hoping to make big profits on wheat. The wheat plants, unfortunately, didn't anchor the soil as well as the buffalo grass and other natural vegetation had. So loose soil quickly began to drift away between the young plants. Long periods of drought made the situation worse. Light, dry topsoil swirled skyward, creating clouds of dust 5 miles high. Winds carried these "black blizzards" eastward across the United States and far out over the Gulf of Mexico. Heavier soil piled into drifts as much as 30 feet high against the sides of houses and barns.

Between 1933 and 1939 more than 50 million acres across parts of Texas, New Mexico, Colorado, Kansas, and Oklahoma were devastated by wind erosion. Nearly 60 percent of the population of that area—nicknamed the "Dust Bowl"—simply gave up and moved away. The Federal Soil Conservation Service and local soil conservation districts combined their efforts to help the remaining farmers rehabilitate the land. Millions of acres were replanted in grass. Rows of trees were added to act as windbreaks and to help anchor the soil. Farmers were encouraged to let half of their land lie fallow, or unplanted, each year, storing water for the next year's crops, and to plant drought-resistant plants in strips between the bare fields. What little rain did fall in this area often came as a sudden downpour, causing splash erosion and washing away loose soil. Farmers were also taught how to use contour plowing and terracing to help trap rainwater.

These efforts eventually helped to restore the land, but during World War II high wheat prices again encouraged farmers to plow up grasslands, and droughts created new dust storms. Finally, in 1956, Congress set up the Soil Bank, paying farmers to retire some of their land to grass. The Soil Bank program was successful but federal funding for it ended in the early 1960s. In the years that followed, a series of programs provided funds for conservation work but not specifically to protect land from production. Then in 1985, renewed concern caused the federal government to establish the Conservation Reserve Program. Under this program farmers are allowed to set aside for a ten-year period land that is eroding three times faster than the allowable rate. In return for a guaranteed amount of money per acre, the farmer must agree to plant this land in permanent grass. The hope is that this time major soil loss can be prevented.

Just as water drops its sediment load wherever the flow slows, wind deposits the material it's transporting as soon as the wind speed lessens. Use a large shallow box or a big box lid that will fit inside a plastic garbage bag to create your own dust bowl. Lay a couple of rocks on the bottom and fill the box about half full of sand or soil mixed with sand. Slide one end of the box into the bag, leaving the plastic open just enough to poke in the nozzle of a blow dryer. Turn the dryer on low and aim the "wind" across the soil's surface for ten seconds. Carefully unwrap the box and observe the results.

When wind sweeps across wide-open land, dunes may form. Sand dunes often take a crescent shape, with the gentle slope showing the direction the wind was blowing from. Dunes in the North American deserts sometimes reach heights of 300 feet. As the angle at the top of the dune becomes steeper, sand slides down the side away from the wind and the dune gradually advances. What evidence can you find that the wind eroded your land model? Did the wind uncover the rocks you buried?

Cold Carvers

Glaciers—masses of ice large enough to last from year to year—also carve rock and move weathered material. Although these icy erosional agents still cover approximately 10 percent of the earth's surface, they have far less impact today than they did in the past. Geologists have found evidence of six periods of glaciation—each lasting thousands of years—called ice ages. At times these ancient glaciers spread as far south as Ohio, Indiana, Missouri, and Illinois in North America and covered much of Europe. How do glaciers move, how can ice carve rock, and how can *glaciologists*, people who study glaciers, tell where a glacier has been at work?

Use a book to slightly elevate one end of a metal cookie sheet. Take an ice cube out of the freezer, set it down on the high end of the sheet, and watch closely. Does your miniature glacier stay put? No. Off it goes, sliding downhill. Gravity pulls on glaciers. Do you see the mini-glacier's trail? The melting cube lubricated itself by producing a thin film of meltwater. The friction, or rubbing, of a glacier moving over the ground creates this same lubricating effect. Glaciers also move because their tremendous weight makes the ice "flow." The next time you're having pancakes for breakfast, watch what happens to the batter on the griddle. Until it cooks enough to set, the batter spreads, propelled by the pressure of its own weight much the way glacial ice moves. Add more batter and the pancake spreads farther. This lets even massive, nearly level ice sheets, like the one covering a large part of Antarctica, travel. One fairly speedy glacier, Storglaciâren, in Sweden, slides forward about 3 inches per day; an even speedier one, Rink Isbrae, in Greenland, travels about 90 feet per day. Avalanches dumping a sudden load of snow may make a glacier slip ahead a little faster. Of course, even then you won't have to worry about outrunning a glacier.

Now lay the cookie sheet down flat and sprinkle a tablespoonful of sand on it. Take a fresh ice cube out of the freezer and set it on top of the sand. After a few seconds pick up your mini-glacier and look at the bottom. Some of the sand will be stuck to your cube. Glaciers pluck up rock material as they move. Valley glaciers, which form high in mountains and move down the slopes, pick up rocks from the sides and bottom of their course. Some rock material may also fall onto the glacier and be carried along.

Rub the gritty surface of your mini-glacier across a sheet of acrylic (the kind that you can buy as a clear folder for reports) or across a scrap piece of glass. Look closely at the surface. Rub it with your fingers. Glaciers change the earth's surface by scraping it. Long, straight grooves in rock surfaces are one sure sign that a glacier has passed.

The Old Man of the Mountain in New Hampshire was carved by a glacier. Glaciers also change the earth by depositing rock material they've collected. Really large boulders may be deposited in an otherwise flat area. Plymouth Rock, where the Pilgrims are supposed to have first set foot in the New World, is thought to have been placed there by a glacier. *Eskers* are winding ridges of debris snaking along where streams of meltwater flowed through a tunnel in a glacier. When a glacier melts faster than new ice can be added to make it advance, its load of debris is dropped. This material, called *moraine,* is a telltale sign that a glacier once passed

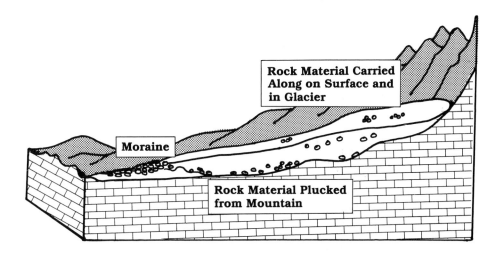

through an area. You'll remember that when sediment settled out of water it became layered—the heaviest material was on the bottom and the lightest was on top. Because moraine is simply dumped rather than deposited, large rocks are mixed with finer material.

In some parts of the world glaciers are greatly appreciated—not because they shape the earth's surface but because they are natural reservoirs of fresh water. Farmers in northern Pakistan, for example, have been making their own glaciers for centuries. First a cool shady pit is found close to the snowline and near a tributary that will feed water into a main irrigation stream for the valley below. This pit is lined with snow, straw, herbs, dung, salt, or charcoal to provide an insulating layer. Then it is packed with seed ice—often laboriously hauled to the site on the workers' backs. This ice is also covered with a coat of insulation, and leather bottles or earthenware jars of water are placed on top. This moisture seeps down into the pit, freezing as it adheres to the seed ice. If the glacier begins to grow, in time the farmers will have an irrigation source they can count on throughout the summer.

Japan is also interested in glaciers as a source of fresh water during the summer months. However, geologists at Nagoya University are using more advanced technology to grow their glaciers. First drift fences are set up to strategically load snow in a pit already containing firn, or crystallized snow pellets. Then bulldozers add more snow, and explosive charges are set off at strategic locations to create avalanches that will drop snow into the pit. Fi-

61

nally, snow melting is slowed by covering the developing glacier with plastic sheets.

Who knows, maybe someday even those man-made glaciers will carve the land. Water, wind, and ice—even plants, animals, and people—these destructive forces are constantly at work sculpturing the earth's crust.

This famous rock is Shiprock in New Mexico. Stretching nearly 1,400 feet above the surrounding desert, it is the neck, or lava plug, of an ancient volcano. All of the rest of the volcano has been eroded away. Shiprock is an excellent example of how some minerals and the rocks they form erode quickly while others resist the earth's destructive forces. Because of this and because the earth's surface is covered with many different kinds of minerals and rocks, the land has been carved into a wonderfully varied landscape. Why are some minerals more resistant than others? What special traits distinguish different kinds of minerals? You'll investigate this and discover the many uses people have found for minerals—maybe even figure out a few new ones of your own—in the next chapter.

Can you name the mineral being mined in this picture? In ancient times it was so valuable that it was used as money, and Roman soldiers received bags of it as part of their pay. Today it's one of the cheapest things you can buy in the grocery store. You've probably eaten some very recently. Can you guess what it is?

Exploring the Earth's Mineral Resources

International Salt Company

Tasty Mineral

Did you identify what was being mined as salt? It's a mineral your body needs to survive. You need to replace this mineral every day because some of it is lost through tears, sweat, and urine. Adults need about 6 grams—a thimbleful—and children need about half that amount. Salt also has many important uses, such as preserving food and tanning leather.

In ancient times only people who lived near the ocean were lucky enough to have plenty of salt. They quickly learned how to collect salt from seawater. The early German tribes, for example, set logs on fire and then threw seawater onto the blazing wood. The salt was left behind when the water turned to steam. A more widespread method was to boil saltwater in a kettle. You can try this. Mix one-quarter cup of salt in one cup of water and stir until the salt is completely dissolved. Pour the brine, or salty solution, into a pan or an electric skillet and bring it to a boil. Watch closely so you can shut off the heat as soon as the water has completely evaporated. Let the pan or skillet sit until it has cooled. Where did the salt collect in the pan? How is this salt different from the salt you stirred into solution?

Salt springs and, later, salt wells were also discovered to be good sources of salt. In fact, this brine was usually saltier than seawater because evaporation had removed much of the water and concentrated the salt. The Indians were discovered boiling brine to collect salt near Lake Onondaga in what is now New York State. Colonists soon took over this area and towns grew up around the new salt industry. Syracuse became the leading producer, and the Erie Canal was built partly to help make transporting salt easier and cheaper.

Boiling enough brine to produce large quantities of salt required a lot of kettles and an immense amount of fuel. Worried about how many trees were being cut, New York State officials pleaded with Syracuse salt producers to change their manufacturing technique to solar evaporation.

This method of collecting salt was possibly even more ancient than boiling brine. The salty water was first collected in shallow ponds where the sun's heat evaporated the water. Then the crust of salt was scraped from the ground. Countries where electricity isn't readily available still depend on this production method, and in the United States salt is collected from the Great Salt Lake in Utah through solar evaporation. The main drawback is that the process is much slower.

Mix a salt solution as you did before. When the salt is completely dissolved, pour the brine into a 9 x 13 inch metal cake pan and set it in a warm, sunny place. Check the brine every day. How long does it take the water to completely evaporate? How is the salt you collected different from the salt you stirred into the solution? Is it different from the salt you produced by boiling the brine? Many of the early salteries in the United States used solar evaporation, but salt produced this way was considered less pure than that obtained by boiling. Today chemicals can be used to remove any impurities. Early salt manufacturers in the northeastern United States also had to contend with frequent, heavy rains. Innovative producers developed hinged tops to protect their brine vats.

In 1886 Joseph Duncan invented the vacuum-pan evaporator, which revolutionized the production of salt from brine. Because most of the air was pumped out, the water boiled at a lower temperature, so less fuel was needed. This method also produced granulated salt rather than large, hard chunks. Today great quantities of salt are collected by this method. Huge tanks have replaced the small vacuum pans. Filters help remove moisture, and giant ovens quickly dry the collected salt.

As the picture of the Avery Island mine on page 63 illustrates, salt isn't always found in solution. Where the water completely evaporated from the trapped brine of ancient seawater, natural deposits built up. In North America it took many years for settlers to begin mining, even though they had long been aware of salt outcrops. French Lick, Indiana, and Big Bone Lick, Kentucky, got their names because historically these sites were places where animals gathered to lick salt rocks. At Wieliczka near Kraków, Poland, where salt was mined for more than a thousand years, the work was done creatively. Sculptured figures of salt form a village stretching through 80 miles of mine shafts. There is a church with a salt altar, a marketplace with salt fruits and vegetables, and even boats floating on salt waves. Massive pillars of salt—twice as strong as bricks—support the mine ceiling. Because U.S. mines were developed when more advanced technological techniques were available, here the salt was carved out with explosives and machines. One of the world's largest salt mines is located 1,000 feet beneath the major industrial city of Detroit, Michigan.

Mineral Matters

In its solid form, such as the deposits mined on Avery Island in Louisiana, salt is the *mineral* geologists call halite. What is a mineral? In the pictures below, compare halite to granite, a common *rock*.

Halite

Granite

Do you see the difference? Halite, the mineral, is pure—made up of only one kind of material. The speckles in granite, the rock, are the individual minerals that make it up. Although sometimes when minerals occur in huge masses, they are called rocks, like rock salt, the term *rock* is usually used to refer to a mixture of minerals with each retaining its own special characteristic. To be classified as a mineral, the material must have formed naturally—can't be man-made—from an inorganic substance. This means that the materials that produced the mineral can never have been alive.

That's why coal and petroleum can't officially be minerals although they are often called mineral resources. A mineral must also have a specific chemical composition and a distinct set of physical properties, such as color, hardness, and crystal shape, that can be used to identify it. If a mineral is hard and durable enough to be highly polished, it is classified as a gem.

Minerals are made up of atoms, the building blocks of all matter. Together neutrons (uncharged particles) and protons (positively charged particles,) make up the atom's nucleus. The number of protons determines what kind of matter the atom forms. This number is called the atomic number. For example, hydrogen's number is 1, meaning it has one proton. Electrons, negatively charged particles, orbit the nucleus at various

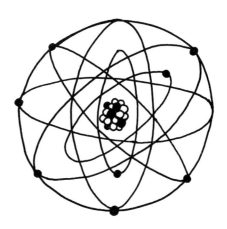

energy levels called shells. In a stable atom the number of protons and electrons is equal.

When the matter is made up of only one type of atom, it's called an *element.* Scientists use chemical symbols to represent the names of each element. About twenty minerals, such as gold, iron, sulfur, and graphite, are elements—made up of only one kind of atom. Most minerals, however, are *compounds* formed when an electrical bond joins two or more elements. The chemical composition of compounds is shown as a formula. For example, hematite (iron ore) is Fe_2O_3. The number below the line tells the proportions of each element. In hematite there are three atoms of oxygen for every two of iron. The formula for halite is NaCl, illustrating that for every atom of sodium, Na, there is an atom of chlorine, Cl. The compound often has properties that are totally different from those of the elements that formed it. For example, sodium is a waxlike, silver-white metal that reacts violently in water, and chlorine is a greenish-yellow, poisonous gas. Halite, however, is a clear, edible solid that dissolves in water.

Crystals

Crystals form when minerals develop slowly from molten material. If there is plenty of room for growth, crystals develop a characteristic shape, mimicking the orderly internal arrangement of the atoms. Because the atomic pattern for each mineral is unique, crystal shapes can be used for identification.

To see why crystals develop only when the mineral is generated slowly, dump beads from an old necklace into a round cake pan. These beads should all be the same size. Shake the pan gently to represent the atoms moving in the molten mineral material. Then stop suddenly. The beads will pile up without having formed any definite pattern. Obsidian, natural glass, is an example of a mineral that forms so quickly that atoms are "frozen" in place. Now shake the pan again, but this time slow down very gradually. You'll see the beads fit together neatly, row upon row. When minerals form, atoms build up a three-dimensional lattice that determines crystal shape and affects many of the other physical characteristics that can be used for identification. Halite crystals, for example, are always cubes. Pour out a little table salt and examine the grains with a magnifying glass. Crystals have long been valued as gems, and in the recent past an increasing number of industrial uses have been found for them—as gunsights, in equipment used to locate submarines and fish, in hearing aids, for improved telephone communication, and much more.

Even though each mineral has its own unique atomic pattern and thus characteristic crystal shape, there are six basic crystal forms, shown on the next page.

Some of the largest crystals ever found were giant feldspar crystals discovered near Karelia in the Soviet Union. Thousands of tons of feldspar were mined from each crystal. In the United States the champion was a spodumene crystal 42 feet long and weighing nearly 90 tons that was found in the Etta Mine near Keystone, South Dakota. Each of these super crystals was embedded in a matrix of pegmatite, a rock aggregate of feldspar and quartz, that supplied pockets of molten material for slow growth over thousands of years.

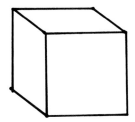

Isometric: All sides are alike. May be cubic like halite or octahedral like diamond.

Tetragonal: Four sides alike and often elongated with pointed ends; for example, zircon.

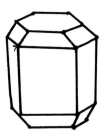

Hexagonal: Six sides alike and often elongated with pointed ends, like quartz.

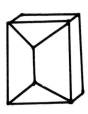

Orthorhombic: Three unequal sides and all right angles where sides meet, such as topaz and sulfur.

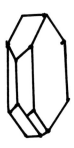

Monoclinic: Three unequal sides but not all angles are right angles so crystals look tilted, like mica.

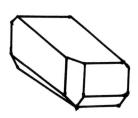

Triclinic: Three unequal sides and none of the angles are right angles—crystals look lopsided and only two crystal faces are visible on one side, as in plagioclase feldspar.

69

Probably the most prized crystals are diamonds. Some of the world's largest and most ancient diamonds were found in India. Diamonds aren't really rare. More than 10 tons are collected every year. However, only about 25 percent of these have the color, weight, and purity of gemstones. The rest are used by industry for grinding, cutting, and drawing wire. A dentist's drill uses diamonds, and so do the bits used to drill oil wells.

A diamond is the hardest substance on earth. It owes its strength to the arrangement of its atoms. Like graphite, a diamond is pure carbon. However, in graphite the atoms are arranged in sheets that slide easily over each other. That's why graphite makes a good lubricant. Diamonds form when tremendous pressure packs those carbon atoms tightly together. Nothing can scratch a diamond except another diamond, and a diamond can only be cut, or cleaved, in one direction—in alignment with its crystal structure. A sharp blow "against the grain" can make a diamond shatter.

A diamond sparkles because it naturally refracts, or bends, light. To understand what this means, stick a pencil into a glass of water and look at it through the side of the glass. Strangely, the part of the pencil below the water doesn't quite seem to mesh with the part above the surface. Light travels more slowly through water than it does through air. So the light being reflected back to your eye from the pencil is being bent more by the water than it is by the air. A diamond refracts light nearly twice as much as water.

Diamonds may be discovered in streams and deposits of sediment, but these have been eroded from the source rock. Diamonds are only found in kimberlite, a volcanic rock that occurs in "pipes"— thought to be the remains of ancient volcanoes. The Kimberley Mine in Kimberley, South Africa, is the world's deepest diamond mine, descending more than 4,000 feet into the earth. There is only one diamond pipe in the United States, at Murfreesboro, Arkansas. Although the largest U.S. diamond, the Uncle Sam, weighing over 40 carats, was discovered at this site, the area isn't considered valuable enough to mine. Instead it has been set aside as a state park. You might want to visit there and try your luck at looking for diamonds.

Grow Your Own

You get bigger by growing from the inside out. Crystals become larger by having material accumulate on the outside. With a little effort you can produce a good-sized crystal of your own from sugar. You'll need:

a one-third-cup measuring cup
water
a saucepan
confectioner's sugar
a tablespoon
a pint jar
a piece of cotton yarn 8 inches long
a small paper clip
a pencil
(If you make sure
all your equipment is clean,
you'll be able to eat
the finished results.)

Heat two-thirds cup water in the pan until it first begins to bubble. Then remove from the heat and add confectioner's sugar, two tablespoons at a time, stirring after each addition, until no more will dissolve. Pour the syrupy liquid into the pint jar. Next, separate one thin strand from the cotton yarn. Tie the paper clip to one end and tie the other end to the pencil. Drop the paper clip into the syrup, resting the pencil across the top of the jar. You may need to wrap the yarn around the pencil to shorten it. The end of the clip should be just above the bottom of the jar.

Put the jar in a quiet place and let it sit. In a couple of days you should begin to see tiny sugar crystals forming on the yarn. Crystalization will happen slowly as the water evaporates. Wait about a week—or until the crystals don't seem to be getting any bigger—before removing them. The crystals you grew are a popular, old-fashioned candy called rock candy. Try a taste. If no crystals formed after a week, you probably didn't saturate your solution with sugar. Try again.

For Identification

In addition to checking for crystal shape, one of the most common ways to identify a mineral is to check its *hardness*. Each mineral has a characteristic hardness value, which can be discovered with a scratch test. This set of minerals, called the *Mohs scale* after Friedrich Mohs, the famous German mineralogist who proposed it in 1822, has been established for comparison:

Mineral	Hardness Value
Diamond	10
Corundum	9
Topaz	8
Quartz	7
Orthoclase feldspar	6
Apatite	5
Fluorite	4
Calcite	3
Gypsum	2
Talc	1

To find out how hard a mineral you're trying to identify is, you could try to scratch it with one of these minerals that has a known hardness value. A mineral will scratch anything softer than itself and be scratched by anything harder. Since you probably won't have a set of Mohs' minerals handy, here are some items you can easily carry along for field testing:

Item	Hardness Value
Coarse (aluminum oxide) sandpaper	9.0
Hardened steel file	7.0
Piece of plate glass	6.0
Steel knife blade	5.5
Iron nail	4.5
Copper penny or brass paper brad	3.0
Your fingernail	2.5
Number 2 pencil	1.0

For example, if the penny doesn't scratch your sample but the nail does, it probably has a hardness value of around 4. Knowing its hardness should help you narrow down the possibilities as you try to identify a mineral.

Using what you know about the hardness of minerals, you can play a trick on a friend. Put a tablespoon of salt into a clear plastic cup. Use a crayon to label this cup *A*. Then put a tablespoon of sand into another cup labeled *B*. Tell your friend that you will be able to tell the salt from the sand blindfolded and without touching either sample. Ready for the trick?

Have your friend put a pinch of either salt or sand between two clean glass microscope slides. Be sure the glass is smooth and unscratched before you start. Then have your friend press the slides together, rubbing back and forth for a couple of seconds. Next, ask that any remaining bits of the sample be brushed off before you receive the slide. Feel the glass carefully. Glass, you'll remember, has a hardness value of 6.0. Halite only has a hardness value of 3 to 3.5. Sand is made up mostly of quartz, which has a hardness value of 7. So if you feel any scratches, you know the slide was rubbed by the sand.

Cleavage, the way a mineral separates—usually parallel to its crystal faces—helps identify some minerals. One telltale characteristic of mica is that it breaks apart in flat sheets. Because it can be cleaved until it's transparent, mica was at one time used as "isinglass" for small windowpanes. Not all minerals exhibit cleavage patterns, but even *fractures*, or random breaks, can provide clues. Clay crumbles into earthy fractures. Conchoidal fractures—curved, shell-like lines— are characteristic of obsidian as pictured at right.

Ward's Natural Science Establishment, Inc.

Color can be useful in identifying minerals such as sulfur, whose bright yellow hue can generally be counted on. However, other minerals may be the same color. Impurities, tiny amounts of other minerals, also make the color of many minerals vary. Quartz, for

73

example, may be clear, milky white, yellowish, smoky gray, purple (amethyst), or rosy pink. Minerals may also appear one color on the outside as a result of weathering and a very different color when broken open. A *streak test*—done by rubbing a mineral across an unglazed ceramic tile—provides the most reliable information. Even though different samples of a mineral may have different hues on the outside, the streak they make will be the same characteristic color.

Luster, shining because light is reflected from a surface, lets minerals be separated into two main groups—metallic and nonmetallic. Metallic minerals are shiny like metal. Nonmetallic minerals aren't shiny and are described by such terms as earthy, pearly, and greasy.

A mineral's *tenacity,* or flexibility, can provide a clue to the identification of some minerals. For example, pyrite, or fool's gold, has the luster and color of real gold, but it shatters when hit with a hammer. Gold is malleable and can easily be pounded into a desired shape. This is one reason ancient artisans chose it to work with.

Certain minerals have natural *magnetic properties* that can both help identify them and aid exploration efforts. Platinum, iron ore, magnetite, and pyrrhotite act as natural magnets. Planes equipped with instruments able to detect magnetism have been used to locate iron ore deposits in such remote places as parts of Labrador.

Mineralogists, people who study minerals, also use certain chemical tests and *flame tests* to help identify minerals or the mineral composition of compounds. You can see how a flame test works by putting a pinch of salt on a spoon and putting it in a candle flame. (The spoon will be blackened so pick an old one—and one that isn't silver.) Tip the spoon if necessary so the salt grains are in direct contact with the flame. You may need to work in a darkened room to notice the bright yellow tint the sodium gives the flame. Either carefully wash and dry this spoon or use another spoon to test a a pinch of salt substitute (the kind used by people advised to avoid salt because of high blood pressure). Read the label to be sure it contains mainly potassium. This mineral will make the flame appear pink.

Useful Minerals

The earth's mineral resources have been tapped since prehistoric times. For jewelry, for weapons, for tools—these minerals were first discovered in their native state or pure form. Then, as the demand grew, great efforts were made to find more of the useful minerals. Ways were discovered to extract minerals from *ores*—naturally occurring combinations of two or more minerals. New lands were explored and settled to obtain minerals. Wars were fought over them. Men and women died sifting them out of streams, digging them from open pits, and hauling them up from the darkness of deep mines. More and more uses were found for familiar mineral resources, and more and more minerals were discovered to be useful. Here are two that made a particularly important impact. They're still important today.

Iron

Pure iron never occurs naturally on earth, but ancient people were able to find some in meteorites (chunks of debris that fall to earth from space). Wanting more, they quickly discovered how to separate iron from its ore by *smelting.* Except for the equipment used, this process remains basically the same today. Iron ore is crushed, mixed with limestone, and heated to nearly 2,750° F in blast furnaces. The iron melts. The limestone fuses with the other minerals in the ore to form *slag,* or waste material, which is drained off. Then the molten iron is poured into molds. In the early smelting process the molds were set around a central channel. Said to look like piglets with their mother, smelted iron was called "pig iron," and it still retains that nickname.

There are a number of different iron ores, but hematite and magnetite are the richest, meaning they contain the most iron. These ores are a combination of iron and oxygen. Pyrite is a mixture of iron and sulfur.

Steel is a harder, rust-resistant form of iron. It's actually an alloy, or mixture, of iron and a small amount of carbon. Some steels today also contain small amounts of nickel, chromium, manganese, and other metals. Metal workers knew how to produce steel as early as the Middle Ages, but it was very hard work. Thin iron strips had to be heated in a charcoal fire for a long time—long enough to burn off impurities and let the iron combine with a small amount of carbon from the charcoal. Then these strips were welded together, usually to make a sword. A good steel sword was rare and highly valued by its owner. Charlemagne, emperor of the Holy Roman Empire from A.D. 800 to 814, had a steel sword. Excalibur, the famous sword from the legend of King Arthur, was probably a steel sword.

In 1864, Henry Bessemer, an American, invented a way to easily convert large quantities of iron into steel. Today this iron alloy is used for everything from the construction of buildings and bridges to the manufacture of automobiles, coat hangers, and much more.

Gold

Gold is better than a credit card. It's a currency people will accept in every country, but you've probably never seen a gold coin. The United States stopped minting gold coins in 1933 and only started again in 1986. Most of the United States gold reserves are still tucked away deep inside a vault at Fort Knox, Kentucky, however. Gold is a precious metal because it's scarce. Geologists believe it formed when liquids and gases deep within the earth rose through faults. Gold can be found in lodes, or large deposits, and veins. Or placers, particles that have washed away and settled, may be sifted out of streams or rivers.

During the gold rushes of 1828 in Dahlonega, Georgia, of 1849 in California, of 1852 in Australia, and of 1898 in the Klondike region of the Yukon, the main way people searched for gold was by panning for placers. You can try your hand at it too. Work outside. Use a round, metal cake pan, a metal skillet, or a heavy aluminum pie plate. Pour in one-quarter cup of sand mixed with two tablespoons of dirt. Have a friend bury some shiny pennies—no fair knowing how many—in the gritty dirt. Then pour in enough water to make a muddy soup. Now, begin to swirl the pan to help the heavier material settle out. Why do you think this step was useful when panning for gold?

Wobble the pan so that you gradually slosh out the water and lighter sand and dirt particles. Add more water if you need to, swirling and sloshing until so little dirty sand is left that you can easily pick out the pennies.

Whether or not they collected a fortune, the people who rushed to search for gold found new homes. Within a year of the start of the gold rush, the California territory had enough people to become a state. The population of the gold-rich provinces of Australia quickly doubled, and the previously little-known part of Canada was settled.

Today the chief gold producers are South Africa, Russia, China, and Canada. Extracting the precious metal is an industrial operation. At Witwatersrand in the Transvaal province of South Africa, site of the world's largest mine, miners work as deep as 10,000 feet. You'll remember that the temperature increases the deeper you go underground. Cold air must be pumped down into the mine to make the tremendous heat bearable. Gold ore is blasted and drilled out. At the surface it's crushed. Then it goes through a series of chemical processes to separate the gold from the slag. The final pure gold is called bullion.

Gold is an excellent electrical conductor. One of the most important uses for gold today is as part of the circuitry for microcomputer chips.

And More

Research is constantly discovering uses for new minerals and ways to make the most of already useful ones. This chart lists some more minerals with their most important uses.

Mineral	Use
Aluminum	This metal is only one-third the weight of iron, doesn't rust, and is a good conductor of electricity and heat. Aluminum is used to make the structural frame for airplanes, automobiles, and ships. It's used for electrical wiring and cookware. Because it's also very malleable, it's used to make aluminum foil.

Bromine   Used in the production of ethylene dibromide, an "antiknock" ingredient in gasoline, bromine was also widely used in insecticides. Most agricultural uses were banned in 1983 because it was considered a possible cause of cancer.

Copper   A good conductor of electricity and heat, copper is used for electrical wiring and the bottoms of cooking pans. Since it doesn't rust easily, copper is used for water pipes, roofs, and gutters. The Statue of Liberty is covered with copper sheeting.

Graphite   Mixed with clay, graphite is used to form pencil lead—the more clay the harder the pencil (number 1 is the hardest, 3 is the softest). It's also used as a lubricant for machine parts and as the electrode in many batteries. It's used in atomic piles to stop nuclear reactions.

Gypsum   This mineral is important to many industries including those producing paints, plaster, and other construction materials. A small amount is added to Portland cement to keep it from hardening too quickly. Crushed, it's added to the soil to help certain plants, such as peas, grow. After it's heated to remove any moisture, it can be ground to produce a white powder called plaster of Paris. It's called that because it was first produced near the French capital.

Kaolin   Kaolin is used to produce the whitest and best china. It's also used to give paper a gloss; in the production of textiles, paints, and linoleum; and in some medicines because it absorbs toxins or poisons.

Mica   Mica was used to make heatproof windows for stoves. Now, because it's an excellent insulator (electricity won't travel through it) mica is used in parts of radar, guided missiles, and many kinds of electronic and electrical equipment.

Sulfur Sulfur is used in plant insecticides and in the production of paper. It's also combined with other chemicals to make many useful compounds. Sulfuric acid is used in many manufacturing processes, including refining petroleum products and producing synthetic fibers.

Uranium This mineral is prized as a source of atomic energy for bombs and for nuclear-powered generating plants.

Zinc Zinc was first used as an alloy with copper to produce brass. Now it's valued as a coating for iron (galvanized iron) because it prevents rusting. It's used in dry-cell batteries and paints.

You may also want to use books and reference materials to explore each of these interesting minerals: borax, talc, calcite, titanium, tin, and magnesium. Can you discover which is the eighth most common element in the earth's crust and lighter than aluminum? Or which is important to making white paint and rockets? Can you find out which will glow if exposed to fluorescent light? Which is used in the manufacture of cosmetics? Which is alloyed with copper and zinc to make bronze? And which, because it's used in the production of glass, was hauled out of Death Valley, California, by mule teams in the 1880s?

Geodes and Thunder Eggs

A geode is a rock secret. If you find a rock that seems unusually light for its size, it could be a geode. Geodes have a shell, usually of quartz or calcite. When you break one open by hitting it with a hammer, you'll find a surprise. (If you do this, put it inside a paper sack, put that sack inside a second one, and put on protective goggles first. You may want an adult's help.) The inside of the shell is filled with crystals projecting into a hollow interior. Some of the very best have been found in Illinois, Iowa, and Missouri. Geodes from Mexico, Brazil, and Uruguay have been found containing beautiful amethyst crystals.

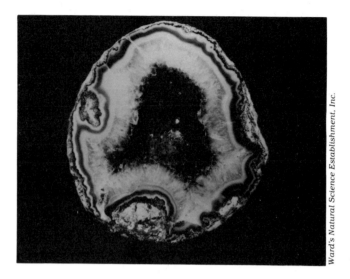

Ward's Natural Science Establishment, Inc.

Thunder eggs are tennis ball–sized lumps that are most commonly found in Oregon and Washington. Thought to have formed inside ancient volcanoes, these dull-looking rocks contain a surprise too. If you crack one open, you'll find a sparkling piece of quartz hidden inside.

Minerals may be found in their pure state, but rocks, mixtures of minerals, are more common. What happens in the earth's crust to combine minerals and form rocks? Will a rock always be the same—or can it change? How do rocks provide clues about what the earth was like in the past? You may not know now, but you will by the end of the next chapter.

The rocks pictured below are granite, sandstone, quartzite, and gneiss (pronounced "nice"). Can you guess what these four rocks have in common? To find out, and to discover a lot more about the earth's rock resources, start . . .

Digging into Rocks

Granite

Sandstone

Quartzite

Gneiss

The Rock Cycle

Forces that are at work deep within the earth and on the surface make rocks change form. The diagram below shows the three main categories that rocks are grouped into by the way they form. It also shows the forces that cause those changes to take place. Very rarely do any of these changes happen quickly, and they may take as long as millions of years. However, because these changes go on steadily and the forms the rocks take repeat, this is called a cycle. The granite, sandstone, quartzite, and gneiss in the picture are

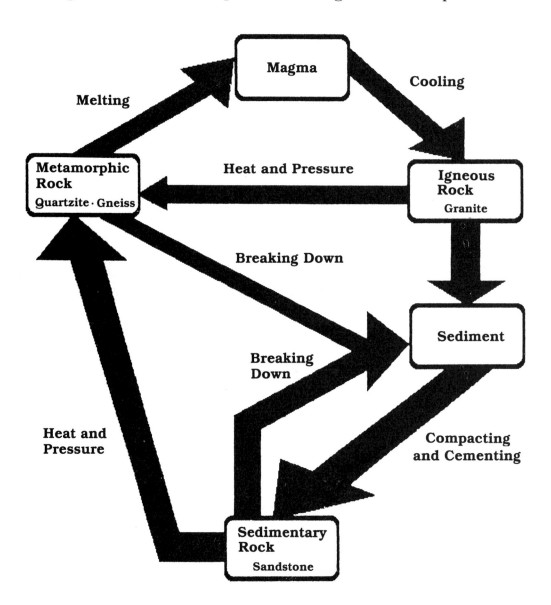

examples of rocks in different stages of the rock cycle. Follow the arrows to trace how granite changes. Eventually you'll come back to granite being formed again.

Granite is an *igneous rock. Igneous* means "produced by fire," and granite forms from molten magma. You've already investigated how the cooling rate affects crystal size. Granite appears speckled because it cools slowly deep underground. The minerals that form granite have a chance to separate and grow into crystals that are big enough to see clearly. In the sample pictured, you can easily pick out the glassy quartz and the white orthoclase feldspar (some granites are composed of a pink plagioclase feldspar). Granites, like this sample, may also contain shiny flecks of mica and dark grains of amphibole. Look closely at the sample and you'll discover that the crystals fit together like interlocking puzzle pieces. This structure makes igneous rocks hard and durable. However, once exposed on the earth's surface, even the toughest igneous rocks eventually weather and break down. The feldspar in granite undergoes a chemical change and becomes clay grains. Once these pieces of the rock puzzle are removed, the more resistant quartz crystals and mica flakes are carried away by wind and water.

When the quartz grains settle out, they build up into layers. The weight of overlying layers packs the particles together. If this happens underwater, minerals seeping down between the particles may act like cement to glue the quartz grains together. The rock that is formed is sandstone. Because it developed from sediment, it's called *sedimentary rock.*

You can make some sedimentary rock of your own. Pour a quarter-cup of sand into an individual-serving cereal box or a half-pint milk carton. Then mix white glue with just enough water to make it runny and pour this slowly over the sand. Add more glue solution as needed until all of the sand is soaked. Then let the developing rock sit for several days or until the top of the sand feels hard and the box is solid when you squeeze the sides. Peel the carton away and examine your rock. You can still see the individual sand grains. Try brushing the sand loose by rubbing the rock with your hand. As in sandstone, the particles are not very strongly locked in. They can easily be freed.

The cementing material gives sandstone its color. An iron oxide cement produces a reddish-brown sandstone. The brownstone buildings of New York City are faced with this kind of sandstone. The most durable sandstones, those that are least likely to crumble, have a silica (a hard, glassy mineral) cement. Some sandstones are more porous—have more openings that aren't filled with cement—than others. If you have a piece of sandstone, weigh it on a kitchen scale. Then completely submerge it in a pan of water and let it sit overnight. The next morning weigh the sandstone again. Any weight gain is a result of water collecting in the rock's pores. You can see why sandstone makes a good reservoir rock for water and petroleum.

Existing rocks may be changed deep underground by pressure from the weight of overlying layers or the earth's heat. Sandstone that is heated becomes quartzite. If you look closely at a sample of quartzite it looks melted. No individual sand grains are visible. None can be brushed loose by rubbing the rock. Granite that is squeezed has its speckled crystals pushed into bands. Gneiss is the name given to any banded rock. The word *metamorphose* means "to change," so any rock that has been changed by heat or pressure is called a *metamorphic rock*. Can you guess why metamorphic rocks and igneous rocks never contain any fossils?

To the Extreme

Schist is a rock that has been exposed to even more pressure than most metamorphic rocks. Its atoms are tightly packed and its minerals have changed to flakes. Mica schist, pictured here, is the most common example.

Rocks That Fizz

Limestone is a rock you can identify with vinegar. Limestone is made up of the mineral calcium carbonate. It usually forms from tiny particles of weathered seashells that are compacted and cemented together. Vinegar is a weak acid. When an acid, even a weak one, comes in contact with calcium carbonate, there is a chemical reaction and tiny bubbles of gas are released. Pour a little vinegar onto a piece of limestone. Then look and listen. You'll hear a fizzing sound and see a froth on the rock.

Marble is the metamorphic rock that forms when limestone is exposed to heat and pressure. Marble may not look anything like limestone. How could you use vinegar to prove that marble and limestone are related?

Sedimentary Rocks with Lumps, Chunks, and Bumps

Sedimentary rocks are formed from the weathered remains of other rocks that have been deposited by water, wind, or glaciers. The kind of rock depends on what material settles out and sometimes on the size and shape of the sediment.

Conglomerates These rocks are made up of the same material as sandstone only with much larger particles. A conglomerate looks like lumpy cement. Sometimes it's called puddingstone. This sedimentary rock contains rounded pebbles one-quarter inch or more in diameter.

Ward's Natural Science Establishment, Inc.

You can make a conglomerate. You'll need:
plaster of Paris
a cutoff plastic jug (such as milk or soft drinks come in)
water
a stick or old spoon
one-quarter cup rounded pebbles
a sheet of waxed paper

Pour one-half cup plaster of Paris into the jug and add just enough water to make a mixture the thickness of pancake batter. Stir in half the pebbles. Shape your conglomerate into a ball and scoop it onto the waxed paper. Poke the remaining pebbles into the plaster matrix and allow it to harden overnight. If the conglomerate has sharp, unweathered rock fragments, it's called breccia.

Ward's Natural Science Establishment, Inc.

Coquina These rocks, like limestone, are made up of weathered seashells—only the pieces of shell are big enough to see clearly. As you can see in the picture, coquina looks like a handful of seashells that stuck together. If you have some shells you've collected at the beach, you can see how coquina forms.

Put the shells in a paper bag and put this inside another bag. Hit the bag with a hammer to break the shells into small and medium-sized pieces.

Pour these into an individual-serving cereal box or a half-pint milk carton. Mix one-half cup of white glue with enough water to make it slightly runny and pour this over the shells. Add more glue and water if necessary to completely cover the shells. Let your coquina sit for several days or until the surface feels hard and the sides are solid when you squeeze the box. Carefully peel off the carton.

Concretions These flat rocks develop in shale or sandstone when particles of soil or sand settling out in slow-moving water collect in rings around some inclusion. The inclusion could be a  tiny fossil or even a grain of sand. Because they are usually harder than the surrounding rock, they weather out and are found separately. Concretions may also form in limestone.

To see how a concretion forms, make one of your own. First work a stick of modeling clay in your hands until it is soft and flexible. Next, roll the clay between your hands to shape it. You may need to divide the stick in half and roll each section separately. Continue to roll the clay until it forms a long rope. Then put a small pebble on a sheet of waxed paper and coil the clay in rings around the pebble.

Signs of the Past

Because they haven't been exposed to the tremendous heat and pressure that affects igneous and metamorphic rock, sedimentary rocks contain clues about what the earth's surface was like in the past. For example, sandstone may show ripple marks, the work of ancient streams or seas. Or cross bedding can reveal that the sandstone was once windblown dunes in a desert landscape. Shale may bear the scars of cracks formed as the sun baked mud millions of years ago. Sedimentary rocks also contain fossils—tracks, traces, and preserved remains of plant and animal life.

Fossils may be impressions, such as animal footprints or the shapes of dead plants and animals whose body parts decayed as the sediment hardened. Mold fossils form when impressions are later filled with sediment that hardens into rock. If you have sedimentary rock in your area, visit an outcrop (an exposed rock face) or a road cut to look for ancient impression and mold fossils. If you live in a city, look for modern fossils—impressions in cement sidewalks. Can you identify what plant or animal made each impression? What can you infer about the earth's surface from these modern fossils? Impressions of winged maple seeds, for example, would only be found in areas with a temperate climate, adequate water, and fertile soil. Ancient fossils reveal that same sort of information about what the earth was like at the time the fossil plant or animal was alive.

This piece of limestone was found on dry land in northern Ohio. Do any of the fossils look similar to animals alive now? What do these tell you about what that part of Ohio was like in the past?

Ward's Natural Science Establishment, Inc.

Impression and mold fossils of tropical plants have been found in Antarctica. What secret does this tell you about that cold region's ancient history?

You can make some mystery fossils to challenge your friends. You'll need:

a cutoff plastic milk jug or soft drink container
plaster of Paris
a measuring cup
water
an old spoon
a shoe box
vegetable oil

In the plastic container, mix two cups of plaster with enough water to make it as thick as pancake batter. Pour the plaster into the box and spread it across the bottom. Coat objects such as a leaf, a seashell, an acorn, a coin, and an old shoestring with the vegetable oil and press them into the wet plaster. Let it sit overnight. Gently remove the objects and hide them. Then ask your friends to identify what made each impression.

When mineral water soaks into such porous materials as bones and wood, petrified fossils form. If this process happens slowly, even cell walls are duplicated. Mix up a solution of powdered clothing starch and water. Then dip in a piece of 100-percent-cotton cloth and completely soak it with the liquid starch. Run your fingers down the cloth to remove any excess and lay it on a piece of waxed paper to dry. Look at the stiff cloth with a magnifying glass, examining how the starch coats the fibers. In a petrified fossil the original material would have decayed, leaving only the hard coating.

Carbonization leaves a tracing on rock. Observe the leaves on the piece of limestone shown below.

As the buried plant decayed, a carbon film was left behind. To

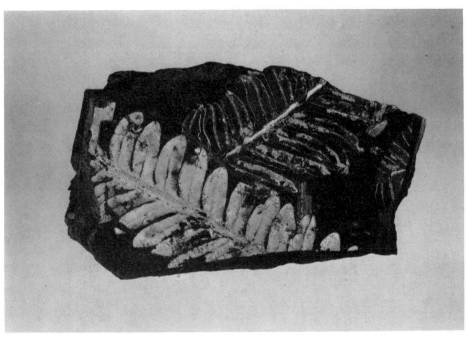

Ward's Natural Science Establishment, Inc.

89

simulate this process, place a piece of carbon paper, carbon side down, over a piece of plain paper. Put a leaf on top of the carbon paper and cover it with another sheet of paper. Use the back of a metal spoon to rub hard back and forth across this top sheet. Lift up the carbon paper and peek at the results. You may want to turn this into a collage by moving the leaf and rubbing over it in several other locations. Or you could add rubbings of other leaves.

Some preserved fossils have been found. *Paleontologists*, people who study fossils, have recovered animal remains from the La Brea tar pits in Los Angeles, California. Woolly mammoths have been found frozen in glaciers. Some of these have even had food in their mouths and stomachs, adding further information about life on earth in ancient times. Fossilized insects have been discovered preserved in natural paraffin in mines in Poland. Others have been found in amber (fossilized tree sap).

Paleontologists believe that dinosaurs used to swallow stones—the way chickens swallow grit—to help them digest their food. These belly boulders or *gastroliths* are rounded stones, usually quartz or agate, and have a glassy, polished appearance. Some have been discovered that are as big as a bowling ball. Do you think dinosaurs with such big belly boulders rattled when they walked?

How Rocks Show Their Age

If you have ever counted the rings on a stump to figure out how old the tree was when it fell or was cut down, you know what one annual ring consists of. It's a light layer formed during the spring and a dark layer that developed during the summer. To determine the tree's age, you count either the light or dark rings, but not both. In parts of the world where there are distinct summer and winter seasons, a similar kind of layering provides a clue about the age of sedimentary rock. During the spring and summer, full, fast-flowing streams and rivers carry big pebbles and particles to be deposited in ponds and lakes. During the winter, while the surface of the pond or lake is frozen over, only fine particles and bits of dark, rotting plant matter that were already suspended in the water settle out. When this layered sediment hardens into rock, it forms *varves*, dark bands of winter material and light stripes of spring/summer deposits, that can be counted like the annual rings in a tree to reveal the rock's age. Rocks 20,000 years old have been dated by counting varves.

A more generalized kind of dating can be used to determine the relative ages of rocks within a series of layers. These three rules are used:

1. All sedimentary rocks are deposited horizontally so the oldest layer is on the bottom. If you haven't already done a settling test to see how sediment forms horizontal layers, try that now. (See page 50 for the directions.) Then repeat the test, stirring up the sediment and propping the jar at an angle to see if the layers will still form horizontally.

2. If igneous rock material has been intruded, it's younger than the rock around it.

3. If there are several intrusions, the youngest is the one that is continuous (hasn't been cut by any other intrusion).

Using these geologic laws, can you find the youngest layer in each of the examples shown below?

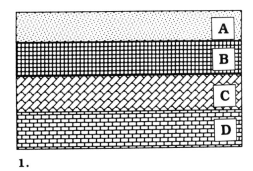

1.

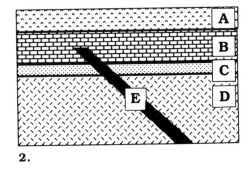

2.

1.A, 2.E

Geologists check the arrangement of different-sized particles in rock layers—you'll remember that heavier particles always settle first—to determine if some layers have been turned upside down. Ripple marks caused by water action on surface layers can also help show which layer was once on top.

When sedimentary rocks contain fossils, these can help date the rocks and order layers that have been tilted or folded. Special fossils called *index fossils* represent plants or animals that were once very plentiful over a large part of the world but only lived during a limited period of geologic time.

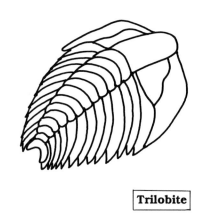

Trilobite

For example, more than a thousand varieties of fossil trilobites have been discovered in all parts of the world. However, trilobites, it has been determined, only lived during a period of time that extended from 225 to 500 million years ago. So if you have sedimentary rock in your area and you find a fossil trilobite, you'll know the approximate age of the rock surrounding it. Do you think dinosaurs could be used as index fossils? What present-day animals do you think are related to trilobites?

Fossils can help date rocks in another way. All living things contain radioactive carbon 14. How much depends on the amount of body tissue. This radioactive material slowly and constantly changes into nitrogen atoms. However, as long as the plant or animal is alive, new carbon 14 atoms are taken in as replacements, and the total amount remains the same. After death, no more carbon 14 atoms are added, so the quantity decreases at a predictable rate. About half will have disappeared after 5,730 years. Using an instrument called a Geiger counter, it's possible to determine the amount of carbon 14 still remaining. Then, by comparing this to how much carbon 14 would be present in that same amount of living matter, the approximate age can be determined. This method can be used to date fossil-containing rocks that are as much as 50,000 years old. After that, too little carbon 14 remains.

Geologists use four other radioactive materials besides carbon 14 to date rocks in a similar way. Some of these materials can be used to date rocks that don't contain fossils and rocks that are much more than 50,000 years old. For example, using radioactive dating, geologists have discovered that some rocks in the erosion-worn Laurentian Mountains of Canada are nearly four billion years old. These are among the most ancient rocks on earth.

Using all these dating techniques to interpret and trace related rock layers, geologists gradually compiled a worldwide picture of the earth's history called the geologic calendar. The effort to find out more about the history of the crust and to more accurately date rocks has been motivated by the search for valuable natural resources. All of the earth's petroleum reserves and coal deposits as well as a number of other valuable rocks and minerals are found only in layers that formed during specific periods of the earth's past or when certain conditions existed. By studying the rock record, geologists can find areas where the crust is likely to contain valuable natural resources.

Geologic Calendar

Here, briefly, is the history of what happened to the earth's crust and what life forms developed on its surface from the most distant past to the present as compiled by geologists studying the rock record.

Precambrian Era (about 4 billion years ago to 600 million years ago)

The earliest mountain building took place. There was volcanic activity and the intrusion of igneous material. Sediment began to be deposited. The earliest life forms—algae and fungi—appeared. Later there were also bacteria, worms, and mollusks.

Paleozoic Era

Cambrian Period (600 million to 500 million years ago) Warm, shallow seas covered most of the continents. Algae were abundant. Trilobites were the dominant life form.

Ordovician Period (500 million to 440 million years ago) Warm, shallow seas covered most of the continents. Seaweeds flourished. Trilobites were abundant. The first vertebrates (animals with backbones) appeared.

Silurian Period (440 million to 400 million years ago) There were widespread inland seas covering relatively flat continents. Honeycomb corals were abundant enough to be used as index fossils. The first air-breathing animals appeared.

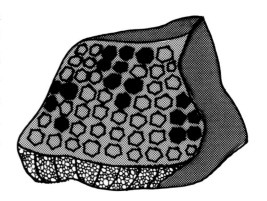

Honeycomb Coral

Devonian Period (400 million to 350 million years ago) Large inland seas covered most of the earth. Uplift marked the beginning of mountain building. Fishes were dominant. Corals were plentiful. The first forests (scale trees) developed and the first seed plants formed.

Mississippian Period (350 million to 330 million year ago) The coal-forming swamps began to form in the inland seas. Seed plants were widespread. Mountains began to push up in eastern North America. Sharks and bony fishes were abundant. Ammonites were common enough to be used now as index fossils.

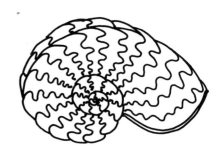

Ammonite

Pennsylvanian Period (330 million to 270 million years ago) Huge swamps that would later form coal deposits developed in the shallow inland seas. Amphibians lived in the swamps, and the first reptiles appeared, crawling on the land. Uplift formed the Appalachian Mountains.

Permian Period (275 million to 225 million years ago) Appalachian mountain building stopped. Reptiles were developing. Trilobites became extinct.

Mesozoic Era

Triassic Period (225 million to 180 million years ago) Vast areas of the continents were above water. Winds swept across huge deserts. Giant conifers grew in moist areas, and the early dinosaurs appeared.

Jurassic Period (180 million to 135 million years ago) Shallow seas spread over large parts of western North America between the rising mountains. Huge dinosaurs roamed the swamps. Conifers were dominant plants. The first birds appeared.

Cretaceous Period (135 million to 70 million years ago) Large chalk beds formed. There were a lot of igneous intrusions and mountain building, including formation of the Rocky Mountains in North America. For the last time, the ocean spread over large continental land areas. The first modern insects appeared as flowering plants developed. Dinosaurs became extinct.

Cenozoic Era

Tertiary Period (70 million to 60,000 years ago) The Rocky Mountains were uplifted and lava flows formed the Columbia Plateau. The climate was first warm, then gradually became cooler. Foraminifera were common enough to be considered index fossils now. The first modern mammals, including horses and whales, appeared.

Foraminifera

Quarternary Period (60,000 years ago to present) Four times—each ice age lasting thousands of years—glaciers covered large areas of the earth's surface. The Sierra Nevada and other western mountain ranges were uplifted. The woolly mammoths became extinct. Humans became the dominant life form.

Useful Rocks

Rocks have always been useful to people in a variety of ways, as weapons and tools, as building materials, and for decorative and religious purposes.

Long ago, people learned to start fires by striking flint to produce sparks. They used sharp stones to scrape skins when they tanned leather, and they learned to make weapons from stones. Chert, flint, and obsidian were favorite stones for making arrowheads and spear heads. They're very common in some areas—you may have already found one. Because these rocks broke in conchoidal fractures (see picture on page 73), pieces could be chipped away to produce sharp edges. So much obsidian, carved and uncarved, is found scattered through the Midwest that it's amazing to realize that it was all hauled there by the Indians. Obsidian doesn't occur naturally anywhere in that area. It's believed obsidian was a valued article of trade. Other weapons that used stones include the slingshot and the catapult. Capable of hurling stones that weighed from 10 to 60 pounds, catapults were an army's main artillery until the cannon was invented. Millstones remained an important tool for centuries. Water, wind, or animal power turned a stone—usually fitted on top of another—to grind grain into flour.

Granite, basalt, limestone, marble, sandstone, slate, and travertine are all used as building stones. Natural faults, or cracks in rocks, were used as a starting point for quarrying early building stones. Holes were bored along the fault and filled with wooden wedges. Then the wedges were soaked with water to make them swell. Eventually the rock would split enough to saw out blocks using copper wire studded with diamonds and other industrial-quality hard gems. Hammers and chisels were used for the final shaping. These blocks—often of massive proportions—were used to construct impressive monuments, temples, roads, and bridges.

Stonehenge on the Salisbury Plain in Wiltshire, England, is one of the most famous ancient stone structures. It's thought to be an astronomical observatory nearly 4,000 years old. The outside circle was made up of thirty blocks of gray sandstone each approximately 13 feet tall and weighing about 28 tons. This type of sandstone is found only in the western part of Wales, some 300 miles away. So the huge blocks must have been moved with tremendous effort. The inner circle is made up of sixty blue stones weighing about 4 tons each. These are thought to have been brought from Pembrokeshire, about 250 miles away. In the very center, there is a horseshoe-shaped set of stones—one inside the other—and a stone marker about 8 yards to the east. Scientists have discovered that the positions of the stone slabs indicate the place on the horizon where the sun and the moon will rise and set about June 21 and December 21, the summer and winter solstices. They also found that solar and lunar eclipses could be accurately predicted by observations in the stone circles.

The Egyptians built huge pyramids of limestone blocks as tombs for their pharaohs and other wealthy people. More than seventy still stand along the Nile in Egypt. The most famous and best preserved are the three at Giza near Cairo. One of these, called the Great Pyramid, is constructed of more than two million limestone blocks, each weighing approximately 2 tons. The pyramid is 450 feet tall (it was originally 481 feet tall, but some of the top stones are missing) and covers 13 acres.

This massive structure becomes even more impressive when you realize that it was built completely by manual labor. The blocks were so tightly fitted that no mortar, a material used to bind stones together, was needed. Finally, the outside was completely covered with white casing stones. At a distance, these made the pyramid appear to be cut from one solid stone. Today most of the casing stones are gone, but the limestone blocks remain in amazingly good shape. The dry desert climate has helped to preserve the pyramids. Limestone, you'll remember, dissolves in dilute hydrochloric acid. This acid forms naturally and causes chemical weathering in moist climates.

The Great Wall of China is another fantastic engineering project, created using building stones. It was begun in the seventh century B.C. Stretching more than 1,600 miles from the southern Kansu province in the west to the coast east of Beijing, this is the only man-made structure that astronauts have been able to identify from the moon. So many workers died helping to build the Great Wall that it has been called the "world's longest cemetery." It was originally designed for defense, but it didn't prove to be very useful at stopping attacks. Instead it became a symbol separating everything that was Chinese from everything that was not.

Roman bridges and aqueducts—an early community water system—used stone blocks set in an arch to support the weight of traffic and water. The arch uses the force of compression to make the keystone, or center stone, and the blocks on either side stick together. Of six ancient Roman bridges still standing in Rome, five are in use, carrying cars and trucks instead of chariots and legions of soldiers. The Romans also built more than 50,000 miles of stone roads linking settlements from North Africa to Great Britain.

For centuries great cathedrals and castles were built of stone. Today many public buildings and monuments are at least faced with stone. These blocks are quarried with modern tools and machinery. First a machine that looks like a locomotive moves along a track on top of the rock, forcing chisels into the stone. Then vertical holes may be drilled and filled with explosives to break away a large mass of stone. Or a jet flame, similar to the tool used to carve Stone Mountain, Georgia, generating temperatures of 4,000 to 5,000° F may be used to pierce the stone. Pneumatic tools, operated by compressed air, cut the massive chunks into smaller blocks. These in turn are sliced with special wire saws to the desired thickness and size. Slate, unlike the other stones in this group, is useful because it separates into thin layers. Over the years slate has been used as a roofing material, in blackboards, and for the tops for billiard tables among other things. Today it's used more for decoration than functional purposes.

How Big Is a Boulder?

Officially, size determines what a rock is called.

Boulder . . . . More than 10 inches in diameter
Cobble . . . . From 2.5 to 10 inches in diameter
Pebble . . . . From .16 to 2.5 inches in diameter
Granule . . . . From .08 to .16 inches in diameter
Grain . . . . From .04 to .08 inches in diameter

If you see anything smaller than that, it's probably dust.

Little, Tiny Stones

What would the world be like without gravel and sand? A lot of streets, sidewalks, and buildings would fall apart. Gravel is mixed with water and cement—a mixture of burned lime, clay, water, and sand—to produce concrete. In how many places around your neighborhood can you find concrete? If a sidewalk, a driveway, or the slab foundation of a house is being laid near you, maybe you can watch how this gray "mud" is spread and smoothed. Be sure and come back the next day to see how it has changed. Gravel is also mixed with asphalt, a black, sticky petroleum product, to pave many highways.

Sand is even more useful. Forced through a hose, sand is used to blast buildings, ships, and bridges clean. You can make sandpaper to smooth a piece of wood. First you'll need a piece of sturdy paper, such as poster board. Spread rubber cement on this, and then sprinkle on an even coating of sand. Let the cement dry for several hours. Then dump off any excess sand and try your sandpaper on a piece of scrap wood or a wooden pencil. Look at the sandpaper you can buy in a hardware store. What determines the different grades—coarse to extra fine?

In a foundry, sand may be used as a mold to cast metal for such things as church bells or ships' anchors. You can use sand to cast a "foot candle." Fill a large-sized shoe box full of sand. Use sand that is slightly moist so it will pack well. Step into the sand barefoot, pressing down enough to make a print several inches deep. Next, strip the wicks out of a number of old candles and melt the colored wax in an old double boiler or in a coffee can set in a pan of water. Hot wax can burn you or easily catch fire so be very

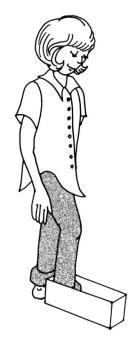

careful. (You may want an adult's help.) For the prettiest results, use candles that are all the same color.

When the wax is melted, using a pot holder, pour it slowly into your footprint. Tie or tape one of the old wicks to a ruler. Lay this across the edges of the box to suspend the wick with the end just above the bottom of the candle. Let the wax sit overnight or until it is completely hardened. Then gently remove your foot candle from the sand.

Large quantities of silicon sand are used every year to produce glass and the silicon chips that are so important to the computer industry. However, there is no concern about running out of this natural resource. The earth has a plentiful supply of sand.

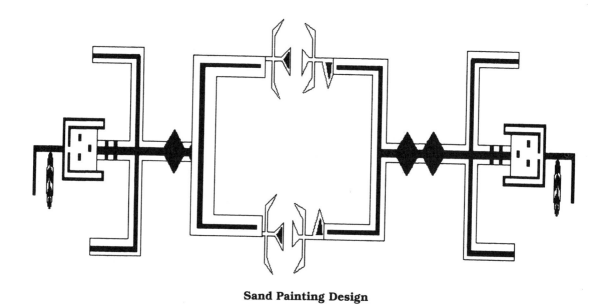

Sand Painting Design

Colorful Sand

The color of sand depends on what kind of rock was ground up to produce it. White sand is mostly coral and seashells. Pale yellow sand is mainly quartz grains. In Hawaii there is a beach of black lava sand and a green beach consisting mostly of the mineral olivine. The Coral Pink Sand Dunes close to Kanab, Utah, are weathered red sandstone. To the Navaho Indians of the southwestern United States, colored sands are special. They even grind rocks to produce their own colored sand for ceremonial paintings. Such paintings were once considered to have healing powers.

You can purchase colored sands in a craft store to create your own sand-art paperweight. You'll need a small baby food jar and two or more colors of sand. Pour a layer of one color into the bottom of the jar. Pour in a different-colored layer slowly to prevent the two from mixing. If you want to add a design, use a toothpick to poke the second layer into the first at intervals along the sides of the jar, forming a scalloped pattern. Repeat layering until the jar is full, and put the lid on tightly.

Eek! It's Quicksand

Have you ever watched a movie where someone stepped into quicksand? They started to sink. If you wondered why, you can make some quicksand of your own to find out. You'll need a two-liter plastic soft drink bottle, sharp scissors, clear wrap, a sink sprayer (or you can work outside and use a garden hose), a small rock, and sand. Cut off the top of the bottle. Then cut a hole in the bottom of the plastic container big enough to poke the end of the sink sprayer or the hose noz-

zle through. Stuff clear wrap around the nozzle as needed to seal the opening. Pour in enough sand to half fill the container and place the rock on top. Turn on the water so it seeps up into the sand. As the sand grains separate, the rock will sink. Turn off the water and let the container sit. What happens? Quicksand forms wherever there is sand with an underground source of water.

Petroleum

LUCAS GUSHER
at Spindle Top
Blew in about 10:00 a.m.
January 10th 1901

Trost

Spindletop Museum, Lamar University, Beaumont, Texas

This is Spindletop. Drilled near Beaumont, Texas, it was the first "gusher." On January 10, 1901, petroleum spouted nearly 150 feet into the air. More than a million barrels poured out before the men could stop the flood nine days later. Spindletop proved that there were large quantities of oil in Texas—and, it was assumed, in the mid-continental area of the United States. Thus the petroleum industry was launched as big business.

Although it's usually considered a mineral resource, petroleum doesn't really fit that classification because it's formed from organic material. Petroleum deposits started when billions of tiny microscopic animals settled to the bottom of ancient seas and were covered by layers of mud and sand. As these sediments hardened into rock, the animal fats changed into gas and petroleum. Finding the first petroleum deposits had been easy. People collected it from pools where the yellowish-green-to-black liquid seeped out of the ground. The first oil well was drilled in Titusville, Pennsylvania, near an oil seep. It was only a shallow well, 69 feet deep.

Geologists have to be earth detectives to find oil deep underground. They look for clues that could reveal where oil is trapped. Drilling an oil well isn't like sticking a straw into a bottle of soda pop, because petroleum doesn't occur in pools. Instead, the oil is between the rock grains just as the water filled up the spaces in sandstone when you tried the investigation on page 84. Pressures within the earth squeeze the oil upward and outward unless it is trapped by impermeable rock—rock with such tightly packed particles that the oil can't penetrate it. Those areas of trapped oil are what geologists want to find.

Fill a wide-mouthed glass half full of sand. Then mix a couple of drops of blue food coloring with one-quarter cup of water and pour the colored water into the glass. Watch closely as the water soaks down, filling in the spaces between the sand grains. Next, fill the glass to the very top with sand and seal the opening with clear wrap. What you've created is similar to a petroleum deposit. When oil is confined in porous rock pockets surrounded by impermeable rock it is said to be in a *stratigraphic trap.*

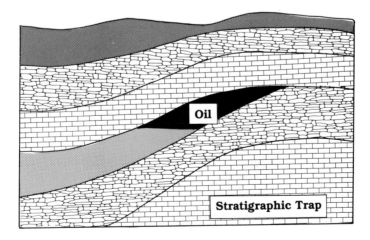

Oil may also become trapped by rock movement along a fault. Porous oil-bearing rock may have been in contact with impermeable rock but not blocked by it. After the shift, the porous rock may change position so the oil is contained by impermeable rock.

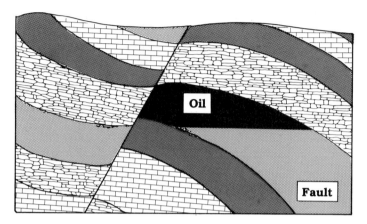

Or impermeable layers of the crust may be pushed up, forming an *anticline*, upward-arching rock layers. Then oil rises into this trap.

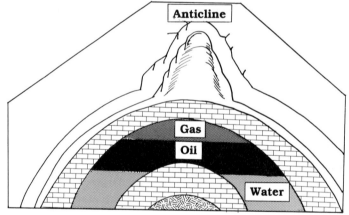

Later, erosion and deposition may hide surface evidence of faults and anticlines. However, aerial photographs and satellite photos can help geologists spot areas that look as though they have unconformities—breaks in contacts between layers of rock. Then seismographs—like the ones you investigated for measuring earthquake waves—can be used to reveal the pattern of deep rock layers. The only way to know for sure if there's oil underground, though, is to drill an exploration well. Drilling a well on land can cost from $2.8 million to $8.5 million. Today many wells are drilled offshore from special drilling platforms. The cost of an offshore well may run as high as $180 million.

Sun Exploration and Production Company

Sun Exploration and Production Company

Tall derricks are used to guide strings of pipe in and out of the well. The drill bit on the end of this pipe has wheels with hard metal teeth to cut down through the rock layers. Although diagrams show the resulting wellbore as a straight channel, in reality it's likely to angle. The bit is deflected a little each time it hits resistant rock. Drilling mud, (a mixture of water, oil, and clay) is constantly circulated to carry the rock fragments up out of the wellbore and to help lubricate the bit. Periodically, casing is put down to line the wellbore and cement is pumped down to seal the outside of the channel. Law requires that the wellbore be isolated this way to prevent oil—if it's found—from spreading out and possibly polluting the groundwater as it's brought to the surface through permeable rock layers. If oil-bearing rock is reached, a special tool is sent down to shoot holes through the pipe and cement casing in the producing section of the wellbore. Oil enters through these holes and either rises because of natural pressures or is pumped out of the well.

If petroleum is found, the derrick is removed and a system of gauges called the Christmas Tree is installed to control the natural pressures that could produce a gusher. The oil may be on top of trapped water. You can see this for yourself. Put a tablespoon of vegetable oil into half a glass of water and stir. Then let the water and oil sit. As you watch, the oil will separate and migrate to the surface of the water. Just like the oil and water in the glass, as petroleum forms it migrates above the water, occupying spaces between rock grains. The upward push of the water in a well is often enough to drive the oil to the surface. Or the petroleum may be capped by a large body of natural gas. Then, like carbon dioxide in soda pop, the release of pressure from above causes the gas to expand downward, driving the oil up. Gushers like Spindletop are now considered wasteful accidents, and oil companies use the tools provided by modern technology to bring in wells under controlled conditions. If, on the other hand, natural pressures aren't enough to carry the oil to the surface, it can be pumped out. Special techniques have even been developed to extract the residual oil that would normally remain clinging to rock particles.

Not only is petroleum used to generate more than 42 percent of the world's energy, but it also supplies basic raw materials for many products from medicines to plastic toys.

Coal

Another unofficial mineral, coal, formed from the remains of dead plants. Sometimes miners find fossils that are evidence of the coal's origin (see Signs of the Past, page 87). Layers of coal are called seams or veins. Geologists have been able to date most coal as being from 1 million to 440 million years old (see How Rocks Show Their Age, page 90), but most is about 300 million years old. This coal formed during what geologists have named the Carboniferous Period, when much of the earth's land area was covered with swamps and lush vegetation. Gradually a thick, compact layer of dead plant matter built up. This *peat* was similar to the spongy material found in bogs today. In parts of Ireland and Scotland, blocks of peat are still cut and carried home for fuel.

Later, layers of sand and mud were deposited on top of the peat. Over millions of years these hardened into sandstone and shale, and moisture and gases were squeezed out of the plant material. Open a package of frozen spinach and put it into a colander in the sink. Measure the thickness of the frozen block of leaves. After it's thawed, press the spinach with paper towels to squeeze out all the moisture you can. When no more drips from the colander, feel the compressed material. It's spongy. Carefully dump the spinach onto a paper towel and measure its thickness again. How much thinner is the compressed spinach? It took 3 to 7 feet of compacted plant matter to produce a coal seam 1 foot thick.

Coal is classified by the amount of carbon it contains. *Lignite*, the youngest coal, isn't mined because of its high moisture and gas content. *Bituminous* or "soft" coal is older and more compacted so it contains more carbon. Most of the coal that is mined is bituminous. *Anthracite* or "hard" coal is the oldest and has the highest carbon content. Although it's harder to ignite, anthracite coal gives off more heat and produces less ash.

Coal is found on every continent, including Antarctica. Geologists search for coal much the same way they look for oil. When a coal deposit is discovered, they use core samples, plugs of rock drilled out of the earth, to tell the extent and width of a coal seam. Press a layer of red modeling clay into the bottom of an individual-serving cereal box or a half-pint milk carton. Put a layer of green clay on top of this and repeat, alternating the colored clays. At some level stick in a chunk of yellow clay. Continue until you have packed about ten layers into the box. Now push a plastic straw straight down into the clay, pull it out, and snip it open length-wise with scissors. The yellow clay represents the coal. Did you get any in your sample? Take five more samples at different locations. Use toothpicks to outline the area you believe to contain the "coal seam." From your core samples, can you tell how thick the "coal seam" is?

A seam must be at least 24 inches thick before it is considered worth mining at this time. Later, if coal becomes more scarce or if inexpensive mining techniques are developed, thinner seams may be mined too. Coal thick enough to mine is called a *coal reserve*. If the reserve is within 200 feet of the surface, strip mining will probably be used to extract it. Heavy machines scrape away the overburden (the soil and rock layers above the reserve) and dig out the coal. This method of mining is safest for the miners but very destructive to the earth. The bare, steeply sloping ground erodes, and exposed rocks give off acids that drain into streams. Starting in 1978, mining companies in the United States were required by law to reclaim strip mines—filling them in and replanting the surface—after they stopped being productive.

To reach deeper coal seams, underground mines are needed. As in salt mines, the room-and-pillar method is sometimes used, leaving columns of coal to support the roof. Later the columns themselves are mined, letting the overburden cave in as the miners back out. The more common approach is called the longwall system. As coal is removed, props and ceiling bolts are put in to support the roof. Mining engineers must study the structural geology of an area carefully to determine how many supports and bolts will be needed to support the overburden. Although efforts have been made to make coal mining safer, there are still cave-ins and accidents resulting from explosions or poor ventilation. Many miners have also suffered from black lung disease. The coal dust they breathe in coats and clogs the alveoli, or tiny air sacs, in their lungs.

Two-thirds of the coal mined today is used by power-generating stations to produce electricity. Coal is also an important fuel for industry. Certain types of bituminous coal are processed to form *coke,* a hard mass of nearly pure carbon. Coke is excellent for generating the tremendous temperatures needed to produce iron and steel. Another useful coal product is *coal tar*. This is made from the gas given off by bituminous coal as coke forms. Products produced from coal tar include pitch, used for waterproofing; benzene and naphthalene, used in making plastics, aspirin, cosmetics, and explosives; and creosote, used as an antiseptic and a wood preservative.

Did you know that coal has even been used for jewelry? During the Victorian era (the nineteenth century) jet, a black variety of lignite, was considered very fashionable for cut and polished buttons and jewelry. Jet jewelry was especially worn by women in mourning.

How to Start Your Own Rock Collection

Although you'll probably find it easier to collect rocks, you may also want to collect minerals. What you find is going to depend on where you live. Even if you live in a city, however, when you start looking down as well as up and around, you'll be surprised by what you discover. Unless you have a friend with a forklift and a large, very sturdy display area, limit yourself to pebble-sized specimens. For one thing, these won't become heavy so quickly when you're out collecting.

Before you start, you'll want to organize this collecting equipment in a backpack. You'll need small, self-sealing plastic bags (so your specimens won't chip and scratch each other or dirty up the bottom of your pack), an old toothbrush to brush dirt off an interesting specimen, a small notebook, a magnifying glass for close-up inspection, and a small, plastic spray bottle full of water (some rocks and minerals look much more interesting wet). You may also want to take along items to use for a hardness test (see page 72), and a small plastic bottle of vinegar and an eyedropper to see if your rock specimens contain calcite. Later you may want to take a pick or a geologist's rock hammer to chip fresh specimens from large rock or mineral deposits. If you do, be sure to also take along protective goggles to wear while you're chipping. You won't need any reference books. Save trying to identify what you find for when you get home.

When you go collecting, here are some places you may want to look: along a stream, in a road cut, on a gravel driveway, up a mountain trail, on a shore, in an alley, and on a playground. To be safe, *never* go in an abandoned mine, a quarry, or a cave. It's wise and more fun to go hunting with a friend. As you find specimens, make a note of the date and where you made your discovery. Tuck this note into the bag with the rock or mineral. This information will need to be included with your display and will be particularly useful if you later decide to trade your sample or to return for further collecting.

At home you'll want to spend some time cleaning your specimens and identifying them. Finally, you'll want to store and display your collection. At first you might want to use egg cartons or shoe boxes. Later you could build a wooden box divided into separate compartments. Be sure to number each specimen to identify it. To do this put a small piece of white adhesive tape (the kind used in bandaging) on it or dab on a spot of white-out (typewriter correction liquid) and let it dry. Then write the number with a permanent marking pen. After the specimen has been numbered, make up an index card for it. Include the specimen's identity, anything of interest about that kind of rock or mineral, and the information you wrote down at the collection site. Store these cards in a recipe box. Since the kinds of rocks and minerals vary with each locality, if you have relatives or friends in other cities or states, you'll want to trade some samples from your area for some from theirs.

What's Next?

You're off to a good start, but don't stop digging. Living on the earth is being part of an investigation that's in progress. You can use what others have discovered about your home planet and keep on exploring. Will you figure out how to predict earthquakes? Can you find a way to track down hidden mineral deposits or develop new uses for the earth's rocks and minerals? Will you discover how to make poor soil fertile and productive? Can you figure out how to provide an adequate supply of fresh water for the deserts?

The earth still has plenty of secrets. You could choose one and make discovering it your career. Your home planet is action-packed, dynamic, and full of surprises. You've just started to explore. So don't stop. Dig deeper!

Glossary

anthracite: Called hard coal, it has the highest carbon content. When it burns, this kind of coal gives off a lot of heat with little flame or smoke.

anticline: Upward-arching rock layers.

Asthenosphere: The area from about 43 to 186 miles below the earth's surface. Volcanic lavas are produced here, and unequal heating of the mantle in this region creates circulating currents that very slowly move the crustal plates.

batholith: Intrusion of magma that covers an area greater than 30 square miles. The magma hardens into igneous rock deep underground and is later exposed by erosion.

bedrock: Uneroded rock material under the soil.

biologist: Someone who studies plant and animal life.

bituminous coal: Soft coal that is older and more compact than lignite. Most of the coal mined is bituminous.

body waves: Earthquake waves that are transmitted through the interior of the earth.

breccia: Type of conglomerate made up of angular pebbles.

central vent: The opening up through the middle of a volcano.

chemical weathering: The breakdown of the earth's materials by changing the internal molecular structure of the minerals.

cinder cone volcano: Volcanic mountain formed by cinders and ash building up into a cone with steep sides.

cleavage: The way a mineral separates, usually parallel to its crystal faces.

composite cone volcano: Volcanic mountain formed by alternating layers of lava and cinders and ash building up into a cone.

compound: Matter that is formed when an electrical bond joins two or more elements.

compressional waves: Body waves that cause particles of matter in the earth to move together and then spread apart. They travel through solids, liquids, and gases. They are also called primary or P waves because they are the first recorded by a seismograph after an earthquake.

concretion: Sedimentary rock formed when particles of soil or sand settling out in slow-moving water collect in rings around an inclusion.

conglomerate: Sedimentary rock made up of rounded, gravel-sized pebbles. It is sometimes called puddingstone.

convection currents: The mass movement of part of a fluid.

coquina: Sedimentary rock made up of large pieces of seashell cemented together.

core: Center area of the earth's interior, believed to be composed mainly of iron and nickel and made up of two layers—the inner core and the outer core. The core is believed to be responsible for the fact that the earth has a magnetic field.

crater: The opening at the top of a volcano.

creep: The slow downward movement of soil.

creepmeter: Records horizontal movement across a fault.

crust: The very thin, relatively light, rigid layer that forms the earth's surface. It is broken into a number of plates and ranges from about 3 to 31 miles thick.

crystal: Orderly arrangement of atoms formed when minerals develop slowly from molten material. The six basic crystal shapes are: isometric, tetragonal, hexagonal, orthorhombic, monoclinic, and triclinic.

cutoff: A short channel formed when a river erodes a path through the narrow section of land between two meanders.

delta: Built-up deposit of sediment where a river empties into an ocean.

dike: Thin, flat intrusion of magma that cuts through surrounding rock layers.

dip-slip fault: Occurs when elastic rebound causes one block of the crust to move vertically in relation to another. This movement forms fault block mountains.

dome mountains: Mountains formed when a pool of magma builds up, pushing up the layers of crust above it.

elastic rebound: Sudden release of energy after a buildup of tension that causes movement along a fault.

element: Matter that is made up of only one type of atom.

epicenter: Point on the earth's surface directly above the focus of an earthquake.

erosion: The movement of weathered material.

esker: Winding ridge of debris deposited by a stream of meltwater flowing through a tunnel in a glacier.

fault: Crack in the earth's crust.

fault block mountains: Mountains formed when there is movement along a dip-slip fault.

fissure: A narrow deep crack in the crust.

focus: Point in the earth's crust where something happens to cause an earthquake.

fold mountains: Mountains formed when the crust crumples.

fossils: Tracks, traces, and preserved remains of plant and animal life.

gastroliths: Rounded stones, usually quartz or agate, that paleontologists believe were once swallowed by dinosaurs to help them digest their food.

geode: A rock that has an internal cavity lined with crystals or layers of silica.

geologist: Someone who studies the earth.

geomorphologist: Someone who studies how the earth's features form.

glacier: A large, thick mass of ice, formed from compacted snow, that flows slowly over the land.

glaciologist: Someone who studies glaciers.

humus: Decaying plant and animal matter.

igneous rock: Rock formed by the cooling of molten magma.

index fossil: A fossil that can be used to identify a specific geologic time.

jetty: Wall built projecting into the water to catch and trap sediment. Jetties are used particularly to protect a harbor.

laccolith: Large intrusion of magma that pushes between existing rock layers.

laser-ranging instrument: Used to reveal the slightest horizontal movement across a fault.

lava: Magma that reaches the earth's surface.

levee: Earth embankment built to hold a river in its banks.

lignite: Softest form of coal.

lithosphere: The crust combined with the uppermost portion of the mantle.

loam: An ideal mixture of clay, silt, sand, and humus. It is considered the best kind of soil for plant growth.

luster: Shiny appearance of a mineral when light is reflected from its surface.

magma: Mantle material.

magnetometer: Records local changes in the earth's magnetic field. Such changes occur when rocks are deformed under pressure.

mantle: Layer of the earth between the crust and the core. It is believed to be about 1,789 miles thick and composed of silicon, magnesium, and iron. Some geologists believe the mantle material may flow like a liquid in response to tremendous heat and pressure but will break like a solid if moved suddenly. Others believe the mantle is always fairly solid and that currents of energy flow through it.

meander: A looplike bend in a river.

meander scar: Formed when an oxbow lake fills in with soil.

mechanical weathering: The breaking down of rocks into smaller pieces.

metamorphic rock: Rock formed when pre-existing rock is exposed to heat or pressure deep within the earth.

Mid-Atlantic Ridge: A mountain chain stretching 10,000 miles along the length of the Atlantic Ocean basin.

mid-Atlantic rift: A large fault that runs like a zipper down the middle of the Mid-Atlantic Ridge.

mineral: A solid, nonliving material made up of only one kind of element.

mineralogist: Someone who studies minerals.

Modified Mercalli scale: Scale developed by Giuseppe Mercalli that is used to measure earthquake intensity based on property damage and eyewitness accounts.

Mohs scale: A set of minerals, named after Friedrich Mohs who proposed it, used to test the hardness of a mineral.

moraine: A load of debris deposited by a glacier as it melted. Unlike sediment that settles in water, where heavier materials are on the bottom, moraine has large rocks mixed with finer materials.

mudflow: A flow of soil and rock debris containing a lot of water.

ore: Naturally occurring combination of two or more minerals.

oxbow lake: A curved lake that forms when a meander is cut off from the rest of the river.

paleontologist: Someone who studies fossils.

Pangaea: Super continent that geologists believe broke up and drifted apart to form today's continents.

pedologist: Someone who studies soils.

plate tectonics: Theory that looks at how the pieces of the earth's crust interact and change, to provide a logical explanation for what forces shape and build the earth's surface.

primary or P waves: *See* compressional waves.

pumice: Chunks of frothy lava.

revetment: A facing of concrete, stone, or sandbags used to cover the outside bank of a river, protecting it from erosion.

Richter scale: Scale developed by Charles F. Richter that is used to measure earthquake intensity based on the amplitude—extreme range—of seismic waves as they are recorded on a seismograph.

rock: A mixture of minerals with each retaining its own special characteristic.

rockslide: A large mass of rock that breaks loose and slides downhill.

scintillator counter: Determines the amount of radioactive radon gas in well water. Before an earthquake the radon level in wells has been discovered to increase dramatically.

secondary or S waves: *See* shear waves.

sedimentary rock: Rock formed from the weathered remains of other rocks that have been deposited by water, wind, or glaciers and then cemented or compacted.

seismic waves: Earthquake waves. *See* body waves; compressional waves; shear waves; surface waves.

seismograph: Special instrument used to record body waves from an earthquake.

shaking table: Computer-controlled device capable of simulating a full range of destructive earthquake forces and construction-site conditions. It lets architects test a model of the building they are designing to be sure it will hold up during an earthquake.

shear waves: Body waves that cause particles in the earth to vibrate from side to side at right angles. They are not transmitted through liquids because the molecules in a liquid slide past each other rather than move apart in opposite directions. They are also called secondary or S waves because they are the second type of body waves recorded by a seismograph after an earthquake.

sheeting: A type of mechanical weathering that causes the splitting off of slablike sheets of rock.

shield volcano: Volcanic mountain formed by layers of runny lava that spread out, creating a flattened shield shape.

sill: Thin, flat intrusion of magma that slips between existing rock layers.

splash erosion: Occurs when soil particles are knocked loose and moved by raindrops.

stalactite: An icicle-like rock formation that hangs from the ceiling of a cave.

stalagmite: An icicle-like rock formation that builds up from the ground inside a cave.

strainmeter: Used to measure expansion and contraction of rocks caused by increase or release of tension within the earth.

stratigraphic trap: Porous rock pocket surrounded by impermeable rock.

strike-slip fault: Occurs when elastic rebound causes one block of the crust to slide horizontally along another.

strong-motion accelerograph (SMA): An instrument capable of measuring exactly how the ground is moving during a strong earthquake. SMA information was used to develop the shaking table used by architects.

subduction: The process of one of the earth's crustal plates sliding under another.

subsoil: The soil layer beneath the topsoil.

surface waves: Earthquake waves that travel along the earth's surface.

surveyor's level and calibrated rod: Used to detect changes in elevation—one portion of land moving up or down in relation to another—caused by movements within the earth.

talus cone: A cone-shaped heap of rock rubble that piles up at the base of a mountain.

terranes: Sections of plates that move together and are acted upon as a unit by the forces that affect plate tectonics.

tiltmeter: Works like a carpenter's level to reveal when the earth's surface tilts.

topsoil: The top layer of the soil, which forms as solid rock particles mix with humus.

tsunami: Giant ocean waves generated by shifts in the earth's crust deep underwater.

tundra: Soil that forms where there are low temperatures year round and little rainfall.

varve: Annual layer of sediment deposited in a lake or pond, consisting of distinct summer and winter bands.

volcanologist: Someone who studies volcanoes.

weathering: The process through which the earth's destructive forces break up rocks.

Index

120